Shaping the Future of Work

Shaping the Future of Work

What Future Worker, Business, Government, and Education Leaders Need to Do for All to Prosper

Thomas A. Kochan
MIT Sloan School of Management and
Institute for Work and Employment Research

BUSINESS EXPERT PRESS

Shaping the Future of Work: What Future Worker, Business, Government, and Education Leaders Need to Do for All to Prosper

First published in 2016 by
Business Expert Press, LLC
222 East 46th Street, New York, NY 10017
www.businessexpertpress.com

ISBN-13: 978-1-63157-401-6 (paperback)
ISBN-13: 978-1-63157-402-3 (e-book)

Business Expert Press Giving Voice to Values on Business Ethics and Corporate Social Responsibility Collection

Collection ISSN: 2333-8806 (print)
Collection ISSN: 2333-8814 (electronic)

Cover and interior design by S4Carlisle Publishing Services
Private Ltd., Chennai, India

First edition: 2016

10 9 8 7 6 5 4 3 2 1

Printed in the United States of America.

Dedication

To the next generations of my family:
Our children and spouses Andrew, Samuel, Jacob,
Ludia, Benjamin, and Teresa
and our grandchildren Mikayla and Isabella.
May they realize their dreams and have
opportunities to make full use of their creative talents.

Contents

Preface

This book is part of a larger project aimed at changing the course the American economy and employment relations system have been on for the past 30 years. From 1980s onward, the economy has been reasonably productive and worked reasonably well for investors and high-level executives, but not for ordinary working Americans and their families. At the same time, many of our institutions that support work atrophied and lost their ability to build an inclusive economy in which the fruits of prosperity are shared widely and equitably.

I've spent most of my career studying ways to encourage innovation and adaptation in the public policies, institutions, and practices that structure and govern work. However, never have I been as deeply concerned as I am now about our failure to adapt to the realities of today—a global economy, advancing technologies, a more diverse work force, a dissolution of traditional employment relationships and accountabilities, and a near void in worker voice and power. I am particularly worried about the mess my generation is leaving our children and grandchildren. It is these concerns that led me to this project. I want to engage members of my generation and members of the next-generation work force in a series of discussions about why we are in this pickle and what, together, we can do to reverse course and put the economy back on a track that works for all.

This book is one component of the effort. It draws on one other major part of the project, the material provided by participants in an online course I taught at MIT in the spring of 2015 called "The American Dream for the Next Generation." I used early drafts of much of the material presented in this book to generate the videos and readings suitable for an online course. In turn, throughout the chapters that follow you will see material provided by course participants. This brings the voices of members of the next-generation work force, which has the biggest stake in these issues, directly into the conversation and analysis. The course attracted about 7,900 participants from the United States and around the world. As in all online courses, not all engaged in all parts of the course. The evidence for all online courses is that over half of those who sign up sample the material of greatest interest to them. So I do not claim that the quotes or data included from the students are representative of the next-generation work force, but they do illustrate how some young (and not so young—the median age of participants was 29) reacted to the issues and offered their views on what needs to be done.

Another aspect of the project is a website (www.speakupforwork.com) that hosts material relevant to the future of work, again with an emphasis on bringing the voices of students, work force participants, and leaders of government, business, labor, and education into a discussion about how we can shape the future of work to better serve us all. I invite you to browse the website and bring your voice into the conversation.

Over the course of my career, like most academics, I focused most of my efforts on writing articles for peer-reviewed scholarly journals and books aimed at my academic and professional colleagues. But my concern about the future of work, along with a recognition that the modes of communication in this media-intensive world have changed, led me to take a different approach. For the past several years I've turned to writing more op-eds, blogs, and short pieces aimed at the broader public that needs to be engaged to find solutions to the workplace challenges we face today. So some of the materials in this book build on pieces published in Cognoscenti, on the editorial page of WBUR (Boston's public radio station), at Fortune.com, at The Conversation, and in other media outlets. And yes, I have succumbed to using Twitter (@TomKochan) and Facebook (Thomas Kochan) gingerly and from time to time to further amplify these various epistles.

I see this book as a sort of living document. I intend to offer additional versions of the online course next year and beyond and in doing so to continue to learn from the voices of students in the United States and other countries. The website will then serve as a repository for updating ideas and tracking progress in tackling the challenges and pursuing the opportunities available for shaping the future of work.

The core argument of this project and this book is we can shape the future of work if we all take decisive individual and collective actions. Three aspects of this argument will be developed throughout the book.

First, business leaders have to make choices about how they compete, and the choices they make have predictable consequences for the quality of jobs created and sustained. Second, workers can shape their future employment opportunities and careers by taking individual actions that will help them be well prepared to contribute to a knowledge- and innovation-based economy and by working together to build new sources of power that are needed to fill the void in bargaining power now present in the labor market. Third, no individual stakeholder—business, workers, government, or education—can successfully turn the economy around so it works for all parties. It will take collaborative actions among these groups to overcome and solve the market and institutional failures that hold back progress today. By doing so these stakeholders can forge what I call a *next-generation social contract* that is capable of generating and sustaining an economy and labor market that works for all.

This book focuses on the situation in the United States. While I am aware that many workers and societies around the world are facing these same or similar challenges, I want to start with a discussion of what needs to be done here, where most of my work and experience and the research of others I will draw on are situated. Perhaps, as it did in the online course, this will motivate people from around the world to discuss how the ideas for shaping the future of work can be adapted to fit with their economies, cultures, and institutions.

I'm an optimist, not (I hope) because I'm delusional but because I've experienced in my own research and involvement in these issues how individual and collective actions can make a difference and produce great results for business and nonprofit organizations and great jobs and careers for those who help achieve these results. This is why I believe we are not just pawns controlled by globalization, technological changes, or any other force totally outside our control. If we take the right actions and work together, we can shape the future of work in ways that work for all.

So I invite you to join this effort. Don't just read the book in a passive mode. Engage with the ideas—agree, disagree, or amplify them with your own experiences and then comment either on the website or via your own favorite media for communicating ideas within your social networks and beyond. Together, perhaps we can make a difference.

Acknowledgments

This book, and the larger project in which it is embedded, evolved out of extended conversations with colleagues over how to deal with my concern about the shortage of opportunities my generation is leaving the next-generation workforce. Four good friends, Tom Barocci, Barbara Dyer, Mary Ann Beyster, and Fran Benson, each in their own way said if I really wanted to improve things for the members of the next generation I should engage them and listen to what they want from their jobs, careers, and personal lives. So I thank them for their advice and for the inspiration to mount this project. My longtime friend and colleague Lee Dyer helped shape, focus, and redirect this effort at key points along the way. I hope that teaching this material to his Cornell students did minimal damage to his stellar reputation. His wisdom and his students' sharp insights are reflected in the pages that follow.

I was very fortunate to work with an outstanding team of young people in teaching the online course that is a part of this project. John McCarthy was our team's anchorman—our technical and subject matter guru all in one. Christine Riordan, Gokce Basbug, Francesca Bellei, Nakul Jamadagni, and George Zaidan helped translate my vague ideas into creative videos, exercises, and reading materials tailored to this online medium. Joel Cutcher-Gershenfeld and Mike Haberman helped create the social contract negotiation simulation that played a key role in the course and provided valuable data reported in this book. We were all supported by an energetic, skilled, and supportive staff from MITx, including Lisa Eichel, Shelly Upton, Lana Scott, and Chris Boebel.

Zeynep Ton and Cate Reavis were great partners in probing how to best tell the story of the Market Basket case I draw on in several chapters. They continue to take our message about how to manage in ways that support good jobs to audiences that can make a difference. Speaking of Market Basket, I have to thank the company's courageous and determined employees and customers for providing such a vivid demonstration of what is at stake when a great company that provides great jobs is put at risk. I feel privileged to tell their story on these pages.

Producing a book is always a team project. In this case, the captain of the team was Kate Babbitt, my erstwhile editor who helped move this manuscript from an early rough draft through the multiple editing stages and in the process vastly improved the quality and clarity of the final product. Likewise, Katy Bertman provided excellent administrative support and responded cheerfully to my many calls for help with technical gremlins that seem to be attracted to my computer. Mary Gentile, the editor of the Giving Voice to Values series at Business Experts Press, has been an enthusiastic champion for this book from the first day we talked about it.

Many of the ideas and experiences reported here are the products of work over many years with faculty members, students, alums, staff, and friends in our MIT Institute for Work and Employment Research (IWER). Robert McKersie and Arnold Zack were especially good at reminding me that history lessons should be written not to reminisce about the past but to inform those who will shape the future. I hope I heeded their advice.

Support for this work was provided to IWER by the Thomas W. Haas Foundation, the Mary Rowe Fund for Conflict Management, the MIT Sloan School of Management, and the Hitachi Foundation. I appreciate their support but remain solely responsible for the contents of the book.

My final thanks go to the students who enrolled in the online course, my MBA students who facilitated discussions with the online students, and the Rutgers and Cornell students who took the class on their campuses. I hope I did justice on these pages to the lessons you conveyed in our forums, assignments, and negotiation exercises.

Prologue

A memo to our children and grandchildren:

Those of us who were lucky enough to be a part of the baby boom generation benefited enormously from an exceptional golden era in American history. From the 1940s to the 1970s, for most of us, as President Kennedy noted, "a rising tide lifted all boats." As children we were told that if we worked hard, stayed in school, and played by the rules we could expect to realize the American Dream of doing better than the standard of living we experienced growing up. Unfortunately, we are not leaving your generation the same prospect for realizing the American Dream.

But all is not lost. I believe that if you learn from the legacy we were given, you can take control of your own destiny and turn this country around in ways that will work for you, your families, and your generation. It will take a good sense of history, a clear strategic vision, and perhaps most of all individual *and* collective action. This book proposes a path forward, one that is informed but not trapped by what worked in the past. We will take to heart Santayana's admonition that those who cannot remember the past are doomed to repeat it. Learning what laid the foundation for our good fortune will help create the modern-day strategies and conditions needed to secure a prosperous and sustainable future for generations to come.

A memo to my fellow baby boomers who worry about the legacy we are about to leave to the next generation:

If we act now, we may have one last chance to avoid leaving a legacy in which our children and grandchildren are destined to experience a lower standard of living than our parents provided for us. We too need to reflect on why many of us were fortunate to have the opportunity to live the American Dream over the course of our careers and why some of us saw that dream come to an abrupt end in recent years. We cannot change the course of events alone or quickly. Instead, we need to reach beyond old solutions, face the realities of today's economy, and, most of all, engage those with the most at stake—the emerging leaders of the next generation.

Both baby boomers who would like one last chance to avoid this legacy and members of the next generation who will need to lead efforts to change the course of affairs need to work together. The chapters that follow are aimed at starting this discussion and generating action.

Let's get started.

CHAPTER 1

The Next Generation's American Dream: What Can Be Done to Achieve It?

Work hard in school, get as much education as you can, play by the rules, and you will do well in life. That was the advice I got from my parents, and it clearly served me, and the majority of my baby boomer cohort, quite well. We were fortunate to graduate from high school, vocational school programs, or college into an economy that was growing, pushing new technological frontiers, and providing ample opportunities to pursue our interests. We were able to live the American Dream.

I wish my generation could promise our children and grandchildren that they would have similar opportunities. But if we are honest, at this moment, we cannot. A majority of Americans now feel that the country has been going in the wrong direction for at least a decade and expect that members of the next generation will have a lower standard of living than ours. (When I use the term next generation, I'm referring roughly to people who are 18 to 33 years old today—the so-called millennials—because they have come of age after the turn of the century.)

Is this outcome inevitable—the result of a global economy, advancing technology, or some other forces outside our control? I don't think so, unless, of course, we do nothing. But reversing course will take a cross-generational effort that involves baby boomers who want one more chance to leave a more positive legacy and next-generation workforce members and leaders who want to regain control of their destiny.

This book is designed to support this type of cross-generational effort, first by starting a conversation with next-generation workers about what they want from their jobs, careers, and family lives—their dreams and aspirations. Then comes the hard part: figuring out what they and leaders of the institutions that shape work and employment opportunities need to do to help the next generation realize its goals.

Is there anything to learn from what made it possible for baby boomers to live the American Dream? I believe so, not so we can try to simply replicate these conditions but so we can understand how to adapt and update them to fit with the needs and demands of today's economy, workforce, and environment. In fact, the basic argument running through this book is this:

> *The key reason for the challenges the workforces of today and to-morrow face is that the rapid pace of change in globalization, technology, and demographics has outpaced many of the public pol-icies, business strategies, and organizational practices that were designed in an earlier era to govern work, pay, and employment relations. Closing this gap by updating these policies, strategies, and practices is essential if the next generation is to regain control of its destiny.*

Preview: Policies and Business Models to Support Great Companies and Great Jobs

To whet your appetite for this argument, let me illustrate two things: first, how outdated our employment policies are; and second, how the models guiding business strategies of corporations need to change.

Most of our labor and employment legislation dates back to the New Deal of the 1930s. That flurry of action was a direct response to the Great Depression and a belated response to the shift from farming to an industrial economy. Not surprisingly, given work and family patterns at that time, the framers of this legislation and the workplace practices that followed had a model of the typical worker in mind. That worker was as a male production employee who worked full time under close managerial supervision in a large domestic firm. Conveniently, he had a wife at home to attend to family and community responsibilities.

Today, in contrast, we have an economy that is knowledge driven and values innovation. The workforce is diverse. Nearly as many women as men are working. People can expect to move across employers multiple times in their careers and in and out of full-time and part-time work so they can attend school and/or take care of family responsibilities. It is not even always clear who the employer is, given the advent of franchise, contractor, and outsourcing arrangements. Yet most of our laws and the regulations and procedures used to enforce them still reflect the earlier era. The United States is the only large industrial economy that still lacks a national policy on paid family leave. The task of updating our policies, business strategies, and workplace practices to suit our knowledge-driven economy and diverse labor force is huge, essential, and long overdue.

The example that illustrates how U.S. business models need to change comes courtesy of a courageous group of employees at Market Basket, a New England grocery chain with 71 stores and 25,000 employees. Their actions highlighted a debate that needs to be raised all across America: namely, what is the purpose of a business—only to make money for shareholders or to make money *and* provide good jobs for employees and good service and fair prices for customers? For six weeks in the summer of 2014, executives, store managers, clerks, truck drivers, and warehouse workers of this family-owned business stood side by side outside their stores demanding that their CEO be reinstated and the business model that made the company thrive and supported good jobs, low prices, and great customer service be maintained. Their customer base cheered them while they had to shop elsewhere at considerable inconvenience and expense. Never before have we seen such a broad coalition of workers and customers unite to save a business from shortsighted shareowners hoping to extract more cash for their pockets. But they did so at considerable risk, because the managers and supervisors who protested had no legal protections under our outmoded labor law, the Wagner Act, which dates back to 1935.

Yet they persevered. Under the combined pressure of this coalition, along with a tremendous outpouring of community support and creative use of social media to maintain solidarity, the board of directors relented and sold the company to the beloved CEO who brought back the workforce, the store's customers, and community goodwill.

I will build on this case at various points in this book because it illustrates both the frustrations many in society experience about what is

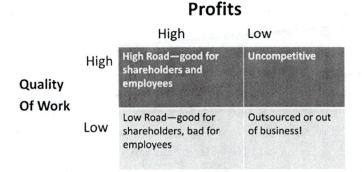

Figure 1.1 America: Which way to compete?

wrong in American business and a positive way these frustrations can be turned into collaborative actions that create change. The reason the Market Basket employees gained such broad and deep public support is that they were seen as fighting to preserve what I illustrate in Figure 1.1, something I and others call a "high road" business strategy and set of workplace practices that can deliver good profits to shareholders, good jobs and careers to employees, and good prices and service to customers. This is what the American public wants to see in business and at work today and in the future. So the public, customers, and employees all rallied together to keep Market Basket from sliding from the high-road to the low-road strategy. Our challenge is to make the high-road model for business strategies and employment relations the norm, not the exception to the more dominant approach that treats employees as just another cost to be minimized, tightly controlled, and disposed of when not needed.

So let's get started, first by painting a quick picture of the challenges and opportunities facing young people entering today's labor force.

A Two-Dimensional Jobs Crisis

The first decade of the twenty-first century earned the sad title of the "lost decade." Workers of almost all occupational and income levels were the losers in two dimensions: the quantity and quality of jobs. If the second decade aspires to be known as the recovering decade, we still have a long way to go. Despite encouraging gains in 2015, the economy still has not generated enough jobs to make up for those lost in the Great Recession of

2007 to 2009 and to absorb the number of young people who have entered the labor force since then. Even worse, the quality of jobs being created is, on average, lower than those lost in the recession.

Figures 1.2 and 1.3 tell these stories. Figure 1.2 tracks how many jobs were lost during the Great Recession and how many still need to be created to keep up with the growth in the labor force since the beginning of the recession. The line that dips deepest in the chart and drags on for years before returning to the level where it started represents today's reality. The other lines provide a comparison with recessions of earlier years. It took a record six years from the start and nearly five years after the end of the Great Recession to recover the jobs that were lost. Every prior post-recession recovery did this at a faster pace, as the lines capturing their growth rates illustrate. The good news is that 2014 and 2015 have been banner years for job creation—finally! But this is still the worst job creation record of any recession since the Great Depression of the 1930s. Let's hope 2014–2015 are the models for the future, not 2009–2013.

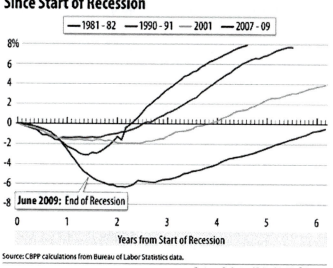

Percent Change in Nonfarm Payroll Employment Since Start of Recession

Source: CBPP calculations from Bureau of Labor Statistics data.

Center on Budget and Policy Priorities | cbpp.org

Figure 1.2 Job losses in past recessions compared to the Great Recession of 2007–2009

Source: Center on Budget and Policy Priorities, Chart Book: The Legacy of the Great Recession, updated November 10, 2010, http://www.cbpp.org/cms/index.cfm?fa=view&id=3252.

How does this affect young people entering the labor market? As late as 2014, nearly 40 percent of college graduates were not finding jobs that would allow them to put the knowledge and skills they learned in college to work. They are what we call "underemployed"—they are working in low-wage retail, restaurant, or other service jobs that don't require a college degree, don't put their skills to work or provide opportunities for further learning and development, and likely pay wages that are hardly sufficient to meet their college debt payments, much less start a career and/or a family. To make things worse, a significant body of research indicates that the imprint of starting a career in this type of depressed labor market lasts for a long time, in some cases one's entire working career. Not finding a career position with a decent starting wage and opportunities for continued learning and advancement imposes significant and in some cases permanent damage.

Young students in the online course provided some first-hand experiences with this. One coined a name for it: "working nomads":

> I think the concept of working is dramatically changing in my generation ([born in the] 80s and younger), and the change couldn't [be] understood by [an] older generation. We want to work at a stable organization, but [those] jobs are vanishing so have to work as an unpaid intern or part-time worker. . . . "Working nomads" are a growing tendency of today's working trends, I think. . . . . So, does this trend entirely change our job structure or [is it] just a temporary trend? I'm not sure, but we should focus on this tendency to understand our generation and today's world.

Figure 1.3 tells the story of the second dimension of the jobs crisis. Look at the 30 years since about 1980, during which earnings have essentially flat-lined. Over the course of those years, the productivity of American workers grew by a healthy 80 percent, but family income grew by about only 10 percent and average hourly wages inched up only about 6 percent. The data in Table 1.1 indicate why the first decade of this century earned its "lost decade" label. Real wages (wages adjusted for increases in the cost of living) either declined or did not increase for high school or college graduates. Only those at the top of the occupational ladder with advanced degrees experienced modest wage growth.

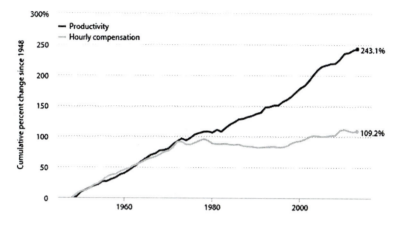

Figure 1.3 The social contract, 1947–2013

Source: Josh Bivens, Elise Gould, Lawrence Mishel, and Heidi Shierholz, "Raising America's Pay: Why It's Our Central Economic and Policy Challenge," Economic Policy Institute, June 4, 2014, http://www.epi.org/publication/raising-americas-pay/.

Where did all the fruits of increased productivity go in the last 30 years? Figure 1.4 tells this well-known story. Most of the income growth went to the top 1 percent or less of the population—the Occupy movement (young people who protested in 2012 that too much of the nation's income was concentrated in the top 1 percent of the population) had its facts right (Figure 1.4). America is now suffering from the highest level of income inequality of any time since the 1920s. Little wonder that politicians from across the political spectrum, from President Obama to Republican Senator Marco Rubio, are talking about the need to address this problem. They and many others, including a significant number of leading economists, business leaders, and even Pope Francis, worry that persistence of this divide will do more than just limit economic growth: it could also threaten the future of our democracy, just as extreme inequality has done in other countries in years past. (See Figure 1.5 for a sample of voices on this issue).

Table 1.1 Total changes in real earnings, 2000–2011

Group	Employment share (%)	Earnings change (%)
Less than high school	8.4	–12.5
High school graduate	27.4	–4.1
Some college	27.8	–8.9
College graduate	23.2	–8.5
Masters' degree	9.5	–3.7
MD, JD, or MBA	1.9	+2.2
PhD	1.8	+3.4

Source: Jonathan Haskel, Robert Z. Lawrence, Edward E. Leamer, and Matthew J. Slaughter, "Globalization and U.S. Wages: Modifying Classic Theory to Explain Recent Facts," *Journal of Economic Perspectives* 26, no. 2 (2012): 119–140.

Figure 1.4 Annual income share of the top 1 percent of the U.S. population

Source: Emmanuel Saez, "Striking It Richer: The Evolution of Top Incomes in the United States," updated with 2009 and 2010 estimates, March 2, 2012, http://elsa.berkeley.edu/~saez /saez-UStopincomes-2010.pdf.

A glance at the earlier years covered in Figure 1.3 suggests that wages and incomes didn't always lag behind growth in productivity. Indeed, from the mid-1940s through most of the 1970s, these two economic indicators moved pretty much in tandem. This fact will feature prominently in our discussion throughout these chapters. The tandem movement of wages and productivity over the three decades following the end of World War II captures the essence of what I will call the post–World War II social contract at work (I will define this contract in Chapter 2). Clearly this contract broke down in the 1980s and has remained broken ever since. We will have to figure out what the next generation's social contract could look like.

Pope Francis	"I ask you to ensure that humanity is served by wealth and not ruled by it. The growth of equality demands something more than economic growth, even though it presupposes it. It demands first of all a transcendent vision of the person. . . . It also calls for decisions, mechanisms and processes directed to a better distribution of wealth, the creation of sources of employment and an integral promotion of the poor which goes beyond a simple welfare mentality." "Pope Francis' Message to World Economic Forum in Davos," News.Va, January 21, 2014, http://www.news.va/en/news/pope-francis-message-to-world-economic-forum-in-da.
Senator Marco Rubio	"Today, the debate on poverty is primarily focused on the growing income gap between the rich and poor. From 1979 to 2007, income for the highest-earning Americans grew more than it did for anyone else. From 1980 to 2005, over 80% of the total increase in income went to the top 1% of American earners. These are indeed startling figures, and they deserve attention. But they do not give us a complete view of the problem before us. Yes, the cashier at a fast food chain makes significantly less than the company's CEO. The problem we face is not simply the gap in pay between them, but rather that too many of those cashiers are stuck in the same job for years on end, unable to find one that pays better. And it is this lack of mobility, not just income inequality that we should be focused on." "Rubio Delivers Address on Fiftieth Anniversary of 'War on Poverty,'" Marc Rubio website, January 8, 2014, http://www.rubio.senate.gov/public/index.cfm/press-releases?ID=958d06fe-16a3-4e8e-b178-664fc10745bf.
President Barack Obama	"We know that people's frustrations run deeper than these most recent political battles. Their frustration is rooted in their own daily battles—to make ends meet, to pay for college, buy a home, save for retirement. It's rooted in the nagging sense that no matter how hard they work, the deck is stacked against them. And it's rooted in the fear that their kids won't be better off than they were. And that is a dangerous and growing inequality and lack of upward mobility that has jeopardized middle-class America's basic bargain—that if you work hard, you have a chance to get ahead." "Remarks by the President on Economic Mobility," White House website, December 4, 2013, http://www.whitehouse.gov/the-press-office/2013/12/04/remarks-president-economic-mobility.
CEO and venture capitalist Nick Hanauer	"We've had it backward for the last 30 years. . . . Rich businesspeople like me don't create jobs. Rather they are a consequence of an ecosystemic feedback loop animated by middle-class consumers, and when they thrive, businesses grow and hire, and owners profit. That's why taxing the rich to pay for investments that benefit all is a great deal for both the middle class and the rich." "Too Hot for TED: Income Inequality," *National Journal*, May 16, 2012.
Warren Buffett, CEO, Berkshire Hathaway	"The Forbes 400, the wealthiest individuals in America, hit a new group record for wealth this year: $1.7 trillion. That's more than five times the $300 billion total in 1992. My gang has been leaving the middle class in the dust." "A Minimum Tax for the Wealthy," *New York Times*, November 25, 2012, http://www.nytimes.com/2012/11/26/opinion/buffett-a-minimum-tax-for-the-wealthy.html.

Figure 1.5 Comments on income inequality

Trends in job satisfaction also track this breakdown in the social contract. Figure 1.6 uses data from the Conference Board, a highly respected business research organization, to track national trends. For the first time since the Conference Board began collecting these data in the 1980s, less than 50 percent of the workforce report that they are satisfied with their jobs. Note that the biggest decline and the lowest level in satisfaction is reported by young workers. In 2013, only 28 percent of workers under age 25 expressed satisfaction with their jobs.

Taken together, these data paint a challenging picture. They tell us that economic conditions exert a strong influence on the ability/willingness of employers to create jobs. These same forces, along with other factors we will discuss later, affect the quality of the jobs firms create and sustain. But employers don't operate in a vacuum. Rather, they operate in a broader ecosystem of potentially powerful institutions—the government, labor unions/consortia, societal norms and expectations, educational systems, and so on—that also influence to some extent the number of jobs and to a large extent the quality of jobs that are created and the quality of the support system for those who for whatever reason lose their jobs. In the postwar period, these forces were such that the American Dream was intact for most people. Since the 1980s, however, things have taken a turn for the worse on wages and other conditions affecting job quality, and since the

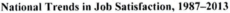

National Trends in Job Satisfaction, 1987–2013

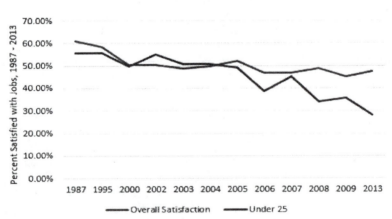

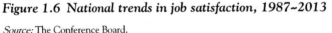

Figure 1.6 National trends in job satisfaction, 1987–2013

Source: The Conference Board.

Great Recession the challenges have extended to a shortage of jobs. Employers are squeezed and, as I will discuss later, unions have lost much of their clout, and government policies and educational systems haven't kept pace with changes in the economy or the nature of work. As a result, it has become difficult to realize the American Dream today, and it promises to get much more difficult for the generations to come unless something is done to change the path we're on.

The Political Dimension:
Is Washington Asleep or in Gridlock?

If a modern-day Rip van Winkle were to wake up today after a 30-year nap, she or he would very likely look at these facts and ask "Why have the leaders of our economic and political institutions let our economy and society slide for so long? Were they all asleep with me?"

And I suppose we would respond: "Good question, but no they were not totally asleep. Instead they have been stuck in ideological gridlock for at least the last decade and in some cases, in particular the relationships between business and labor leaders, for even longer. The sad reality is the country is more divided politically today than at any time perhaps since the 1930s."

Rip's equivalent might then ask, "But what about all the hope I've read about with the election of America's first African American president in 2008? Wasn't that a historic achievement and a marker of greater things to come?" The answer to this equally astute observation would be yes, many of us thought so. That was especially true of young people. They were a powerful force in helping to elect Barack Obama. Sixty-six percent of young voters supported him. Many worked hard on his campaign, and many thought that the combination of the economic crisis he inherited and the positive energy the election gave to the nation would produce transformative changes in policies and practice.[1] Unfortunately, the gridlock not only continued, it got worse. Republicans in Congress

---

[1] Scott Keeter, Juliana Horowitz, and Alec Tyson, "Young Voters in the 2008 Election," Pew Research Center, November 13, 2008, http://www.pewresearch.org /2008/11/13/young-voters-in-the-2008-election/.

blocked nearly everything but the president's compromise economic stimulus package, which avoided the total financial and economic collapse of the banking system and sparked a partial recovery.

So today most young people, indeed most people of all ages, are disillusioned with all politicians—Republicans, Democrats, the president, and especially the do-nothing Congress. A majority (52 percent) of millennials would replace all members of Congress if given the chance, and 47 percent would replace the president.[2] Gallup and other polling services similarly report that confidence in most American institutions has fallen to all-time low levels. Congress gets only a 10 percent confidence rating, organized labor gets about 20 percent, and big business gets 22 percent.[3] Other polls indicate that the majority of Americans share the view that the next generation is destined to experience a lower standard of living than their parents.[4]

Destiny or Opportunity?

So I have covered the bad news, the jobs crisis young workers face as they enter the labor market today and their lack of faith in the leaders and institutions that govern work and employment. But with crisis comes opportunity. Indeed, one bit of good news is that the chorus of diverse voices noted in Figure 1.5 voicing concerns over income inequality suggests that we may be at a point where people, like those courageous Market Basket employees and customers, are ready to do something to address these issues. In fact, over the course of 2015 a few glimmers of hope emerged with companies such as Walmart, McDonald's, and others announcing their intentions to raise wages above the required minimum wage. Regardless of whether one attributes their

---

[2] John Della Volpe, "IOP Releases New Fall Poll, 5 Key Findings and Trends in Millennial Viewpoints," Harvard University Institute of Politics, December 4, 2013, http://www.hks.harvard.edu/news-events/news/articles/millennial-viewpoints.

[3] "Confidence in Institutions," Gallup.com, n.d., http://www.gallup.com/poll /1597/confidence-institutions.aspx#1.

[4] Elizabeth Mendes, "In U.S., Optimism for Youth Reaches an All-Time Low," Gallup.com, May 2, 2011, http://www.gallup.com/poll/147350/optimism-future-youth-reaches-time-low.aspx.

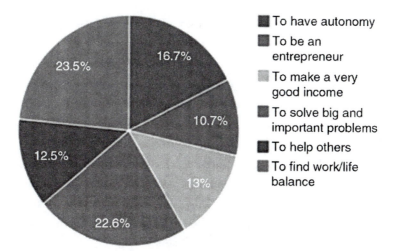

Figure 1.7 Students' aspirations regarding work

Source: Student responses to survey administered through the online course "The American Dream for the Next Generation," MIT Sloan School of Management.

actions to a somewhat tightening labor market or a response to pressures from strikes of fast-food workers and national protests, these are good first steps in the right direction. Let's hope there will be more to come.

A second reason for hope comes from the motivations and aspirations of young people themselves, reinforced by the views expressed by many students in the online class. While they may be disillusioned with American politicians, many are still positive about their own futures and are motivated to address the big problems they and others face at work, in their families, and in society. Take a look, for example, at how students ranked their goals and aspirations for their future jobs.

At the start of the course, I asked participants to rank order their aspirations/priorities for work. The data in Figure 1.7 show that participants want to address big problems at work and at the same time have a sensible work-life balance. While doing well financially is also important, these data, like the findings of other surveys of young and more experienced workers, show it is not at the top of the list.

The wide distribution of responses suggests that no single aspiration dominates. Qualitative comments reinforced this view. This extended quote from a young woman illustrates how she (and she seems to speak for others) sees these different aspirations fitting together:

My dream includes a job where I do important work (working in health care data analytics)—something that gives back to the community. . . . I dream of having a work/life balance that melds together. . . . I hope that I'm able to utilize technology to make work more accessible and eventually have the option to work from home. I do hope to be able to find a company that has a retirement plan where the company contributes some percentage to the plan. In some regards, I hope to have some of the same benefits that my parents had—health insurance, retirement plans, etc. Most importantly, I want to have passion for my work, I want my work to help people and I hope to make a decent living while making the generations before me proud.

Another young woman made a similar point:

I selected that I wanted autonomy out of working. I want flexibility—I want to work hard, but I also want to do many different projects and make various amounts of money doing so, while sometimes taking breaks from working at all that are more than just the 2 weeks provided in a year.

These data and comments suggest that members of today and tomorrow's workforce share many of the same concerns of prior generations, perhaps with a higher weight on having an impact and having adequate flexibility to integrate their work and personal lives. Sloan School MBAs who took the on-campus version of the course in order to engage with the next-generation workforce interpreted these data to suggest that as managers they will need to listen to their employees, engage them in solving problems that really matter to the organization and to society, and to be flexible in how, when, and where people work so they can both be productive and attend to personal and family affairs.

Opportunities for the Taking

So the labor force of the future is ready to take on the challenges they are inheriting. Our responsibility is to give them the opportunities to do so. We need to listen to the voices of the next generation—to learn what their dreams and aspirations are and what they are prepared to do to realize them. And we have to hear from those who have experienced the demise of the American Dream and understand not only what made that dream durable for several decades but also what caused it to end so abruptly. Finally, we need to engage leaders of business, government, labor, and education in a dialogue, indeed in a negotiation, about their interests and what they are prepared to do to get the economy and the labor market moving in directions that work for all.

What Can Be Done? Lessons from Three Decades of Research and Experience

The ideas for what I think needs to be done, outlined below, come from over 30 years of research and direct involvement in the worlds of work and employment relations. Over this time my research, teaching, and work with government agencies, companies, and unions has had a singular theme: the search for innovations that improve the performance of our economy and the quality of work and family life. I will draw on lessons learned from these experiences in the chapters that follow. I present these ideas here not as final solutions but as thought provokers and conversation starters. The goal is to encourage you to engage in this discussion and in doing so widen the circle of voices calling for change and working actively to make good things happen.

Some might argue that globalization and technological change or some other force of nature inevitably means that recent trends will continue. I would agree that this will be the case if we let the status quo continue unchallenged. But I don't believe this is inevitable—not if we act now in well-informed, coordinated, and strategic ways.

Yes, globalization and advances in technology are part of the forces at work here. But they are not really anything new. Similar disruptions and a similar need for fundamental changes in policies, institutions, and practices were experienced when technological and economic advances ushered in the transition from an agricultural to an industrial economy in the early years of the twentieth century. During that transition, too, it was a long time before changes were put in place that allowed the workforce to adjust and benefit from the new economy. Today we are well into another transition—*from an industrial economy to an innovation-and knowledge-based economy*—that is playing out on a global stage with perhaps even more far-reaching effects than the previous transition.

As in the early twentieth century, institutional inertia and political stalemate has resulted in a mismatch between changes in the economy, the workforce, and the world of work and the policies, governance arrangements, institutions, and practices that govern work and employment relationships. Our task—indeed, our opportunity—is to create a better match.

The Foundation: Lifelong Education for All

What will it take to change this? For a start, nothing short of a fundamental set of changes in how we get educated, when we get educated, and who gets educated. The mantra has to be not quite (but almost) cradle-to-grave education for all. The rhetoric about lifelong learning will need to become a reality if the workforce of the future is to compete on a global stage. And it has to start very early in life. There is clear and convincing evidence that investments in pre-kindergarten education pay off in the form of less crime, higher graduation rates, and greater earning potential. It is encouraging to see a consensus building around the need to broaden access to early childhood, pre-kindergarten education in such diverse places as New York, Oklahoma, and Georgia.

Then we have to keep up the pressure for innovation and change in elementary and secondary schools. The "Race to the Top" incentives and requirements imposed by the Obama administration have spurred more innovation in public schools and more collaboration than ever between teachers, their unions, and school administrators who are focused on improving student achievement and school performance. Efforts are currently under way to expand these collaborative efforts in Massachusetts, and the hope is that this initiative will serve as a model for the rest of the country.

In his 2014 and 2015 State of the Union addresses, President Obama called for increased financial support and better coordination and improved results in the technical training provided to high school graduates and current members of the workforce through community colleges and vocational schools and allied institutions. He went on to say "and we know how to do this." He's right. We've learned a great deal about how to make these workforce development programs work—by getting employers in a community or industry to band together, work with these schools, provide on-the-job and classroom learning opportunities, and then provide jobs and career advancement opportunities to graduates. Making the funding of these programs contingent on showing that these features are in place would go a long way toward spreading high-quality programs across the country and eliminating any skill gaps business says it now faces.

Then we come to that highly expensive yet valuable asset called a college degree. American universities remain one of our national treasures—institutions that are still the best in the world. The problems are that they are beyond reach for too many and that debt burdens limit the ability of too many graduates to enjoy the benefits a college degree should provide. But we have fortuitous opportunities unfolding in the form of universities around the world that are anxious to experiment with various forms of online or distance-learning media. The challenge lies in translating the initial burst of innovation in online university courses into sustainable models that in fact provide access to lower-cost and higher-quality college experiences for students around the world. The online course that I'm drawing on here is just one small experiment along these lines. Let's get many others in process and watch and learn from them as well.

These are the investments in education that business, government, labor, and educational institutions will need to make on a large scale to build the human and social capital American employers and workers need in order to be competitive in global markets. They are also investments that individuals will need to make on a lifelong—or at least a career-long— basis. Without a world-class education and world-class capabilities, individual workers will find it hard to compete with lower-cost workers in other countries and employers will be reluctant to invest in American jobs.

Using Technology to Complement and Support Work

At the dawn of the industrial revolution in Britain, major technological advances threatened the livelihood of those who worked in the home-based weaving industry. This led some workers, who became known as

Luddites, to attempt to destroy the new machines. Many technological scares of this type have come and gone over the years, always displacing some workers. These changes disrupt some individuals and their families, but they eventually spur further economic growth and create new job opportunities for workers with the right skills. We are facing this kind of situation in the wake of current and likely future advances in digital technologies.

We will need to embrace advances in technology while we work to assure that they function to complement and not eviscerate work. Our mantra will need to be that it is "people who give wisdom to these machines," to borrow a Japanese phrase. Some experts predict, with good reason, that the coming wave of digital technologies will eliminate large numbers of good jobs. They are right, just as generations before ours worried about similar advances in technologies that freed people like me from farm labor; automated large numbers of difficult, repetitive, and sometimes dangerous production jobs; and transformed or eliminated office and clerical jobs such as chart-room workers in health care. Our challenge is to win the race with, not against, new technologies by inventing new ways to use them and by training workers and modifying work systems in ways that enhance the likelihood that technological investments will realize their full potential. In the best health care organizations, such as, for example, Kaiser Permanente, as technology changed how work was done, chart-room clerical workers were trained and transferred to new jobs that used electronic medical records technologies to promote preventive care and remind patients to get regular checkups.

We need to bring this type of new mindset to would-be inventors and designers of next-generation technologies. For too long, engineers have been trained to focus primarily on how to cut labor costs. While this has its benefits, so too would incentives to invent and develop new technologies— indeed, new entrepreneurial organizations—that use the skills of creative, dedicated people to tackle the globe's greatest environmental and human problems. Innovation and entrepreneurship are critical to job creation. The key is to make this a priority in our university, government, and private-sector laboratories and educational programs. If we combine this initiative with lifelong education programs and creative ideas for structuring work (discussed in later chapters), I'm confident that we will win the race with the new machines and put them to good use for humankind. I certainly prefer typing these words in a warm house with a cup of coffee by my side to having to go out on cold dark winter mornings to milk cows and clean their stalls!

Good Businesses and Good Jobs

Let me be blunt and clear. The values and business strategies that have dominated in most American corporations in recent decades will need to change in big ways if the next-generation workforce is to thrive and the environment is to be saved. For the past several decades, American business has narrowed its focus to a singular objective: maximizing short-term shareholder value. Some have labeled this the "financialization" of the American economy, arguing that pleasing Wall Street has essentially become the top priority of U.S. firms. Business must be challenged to go beyond a focus on maximizing short-term shareholder interests to refocus on a more balanced set of objectives that involve people and the planet as well as profits. This will require overcoming the prevailing teaching about the role of the corporation that has dominated economics and business school curricula for the past two decades. An entire generation of managers and executives has been indoctrinated with the view that their primary, if not sole, responsibility is to attend to shareholder interests and, even worse, attend to and shape their own compensation and rewards to be aligned with short-term shareholder value.

It will also require a concerted effort to rebalance power in organizational decision making. Corporate norms don't rise or fall simply because of good intentions. Power also matters. How this shift in power will occur will be a major question for discussion and a major challenge for those who have the biggest stake in the future (an issue I tackle in the section that follows).

The good news is that we have learned how to do this directly from the businesses that have bucked this trend and focused on managing their affairs in ways that produce good financial results and good jobs and career opportunities. Every industry has its favorite examples—in the airline industry, it might be Southwest; in retail, it might be Costco; in software development, it might be SAS; in health care, it might be

Kaiser Permanente. As noted earlier, the CEO of Market Basket, Arthur T. Demoulas, has now become the poster child for advocating what have been called "high-road" or "high-performance" strategies and employment practices that work for multiple stakeholders. You may work for an organization like this. We need to learn what makes these examples successful for all stakeholders so we then can get on with the task of turning them into the norm rather than the exception.

Worker Power—But Not Just Your Father's Unions

You might be surprised, but in what follows I will argue strongly that the next generation will need its own sources of bargaining power to regain control of its destiny. In the post–World War II era it was labor unions and collective bargaining that gave large number of workers the power needed to improve working conditions, advance their standard of living, and build a strong middle class. Union advocates like to remind us (correctly) that they brought us the weekend and many other benefits we take for granted at work today. Most young people today have no knowledge of and perhaps little reason to even think about unions as anything other than some relic of a bygone era. Yet as we will see, collective actions on the part of young workers will be necessary if they are to turn the country around to meet their aspirations and expectations for good jobs, careers, and family lives.

But it can't be just your father's or grandfather's labor movement—it will need to be a more nimble, flexible, and less constrained set of networks and organizations that can empower workers to find good jobs and discipline employers to meet their expectations while also providing opportunities for employees to update their capabilities throughout their working lives. Indeed, one of the greatest opportunities and needs facing the next-generation workforce is to invent these new forms of advocacy, voice, representation, and support. As part of this project, we will explore experience to date of using worker-centered apps that rate employers and jobs on the qualities young workers value most—and identify which employers to avoid because they come up short on these qualities. This could be one new source of bargaining power for the new tech-savvy and mobile generation. Others will need to be invented as well.

This is not to say that all the strategies labor has used need to be abandoned. History suggests that doing so would only lead us to reinvent them at some point later on. And in fact existing unions and professional associations and a variety of other worker advocacy groups are already developing and incubating new approaches and combining them with tried and true methods from the past. The key is to inform the current generation of what worked before, what lessons past experiences hold for the future, and then let a thousand flowers bloom.

Government as a Catalyst for and Complement to Innovation and Good Jobs

What role for government? One of the key lessons from our history is that, to paraphrase 1980s speaker of the house Tip O'Neill, *all innovations are local*. (He was an old Boston politician and his exact phrase was "all politics are local.")

Almost all federal policies, including the cornerstones of the labor legislation passed as part of President Roosevelt's New Deal in the 1930s, were based on innovations that first were developed, tested, and carefully studied in state and local governments and/or the private sector. The good news is that a tremendous storehouse of innovation has emerged and been tested at these local levels of the economy in recent years. The task now is to wake up, indeed shake up, national policy makers who are in a position to put in place laws and guidelines that are well matched to the needs of the next-generation workforce and economy.

The key is to make government a catalyst and a complement, not an obstacle, to innovation, change, and fairness in work and employment relationships. This is not rocket science, but it will require a groundswell of voices from the next-generation workforce and allies in business, labor, and education who want to step up to these challenges and opportunities. Nothing short of a wholesale set of changes in legislation and enforcement strategies and active cooperation on the part of government policy officials and the commitment of those on the front lines of business, labor, and education to enact these changes in good faith will do the trick.

As one of the examples used at the beginning of this chapter suggested, a top priority will be to end the embarrassing situation of being the last highly developed economy and democracy to provide parents with the supports they need to meet their dual work and family responsibilities. From there we can work on updating wage and hours laws, labor relations laws, and other outmoded policies. And we can insist that government practice what it preaches by requiring government contractors who supply goods and services made in the United States and abroad to pay fair and acceptable wages and comply with accepted employment standards. An increase in the nation's minimum wage is also long overdue, as is demonstrated consistently in polling data and in proactive states and cities that have acted to increase their minimums while Washington remains deadlocked on this and other employment issues.

How to Make This Happen?

We need to build on what we have learned about what works and what is broken in American workplaces, but information and even new ideas are only starting points for producing change. We need to alter the political discourse and build a broad coalition of voices and interest groups calling for changes that work for their specific needs and interests and for the common good. And we need to keep on innovating—bringing new ideas forward that are not chained to past practices, organizational arrangements, or traditions. Call this a "crowdsourcing" approach, if you will, or whatever new ways work for generating ideas from our collective wisdom.

This requires getting these different voices and interest group leaders to engage—perhaps to reengage—with each other in honest dialogue. Perhaps out of such discussions would emerge a common narrative—a vision for the future that otherwise divergent groups might rally around and use to drive change. This used to happen when labor was stronger and business leaders had a broader view of their roles and responsibilities. Together they forged and sustained the postwar social contract. But over time, sad to say, cross-group dialogue largely stopped as business, labor, youth, and other groups all retreated into comfortable conversations with themselves. Now even the media caters to these narrow constituencies. Fox News and the *Wall Street Journal*'s editorials tell conservatives and Tea Party advocates and anyone who opposes President Obama just what they want to hear and report current events through their political filters. So too do the host of more liberal-leaning blogs, think tanks, and journals. It is time to reengage across interest group lines and across generations.

I created an exercise to support this type of dialogue and tried it out in the online course. Students were assigned to serve as representatives of one of four next-generation groups: the workforce, business, government, or education. Their task was to negotiate the "Next Generation Social Contract." I will report the results of these initial negotiations in Chapter 6 and I have made this exercise available on our website www.speakupforwork.com. I invite you to download it and invite others to join you in multiparty negotiations in your community. See if you can reach consensus on the features of a new social contract that is attuned to the needs and interests of today and tomorrow's workforce, economy, and society.

Hopeful Signs

Is this just a pie-in-the-sky thinking or is progress possible? I'm optimistic. American society has responded to such crises before; it has a well-earned reputation for being a collection of pragmatic innovators rather than a group of ideological antagonists.

Another positive sign is the uptick in interest in entrepreneurship among students I encounter and teach at MIT and hear from around the country. Many in the current wave of hopeful entrepreneurs aspire to build mission-driven organizations that address significant social and/or environmental challenges in addition to experiencing financial success. This is extremely important and exciting, given that we know that new firms are an important source of innovation, new jobs, and business norms. Supporting this new wave of entrepreneurship will be an important part of how the next generation invents a new social contract that is appropriately matched to current realities.

As before, out of crisis will come opportunity and out of necessity will come invention. The crisis is clear and the opportunities are there for the taking. But first we have to understand the lessons from history so that we heed Santayana's warning ("Those who do not remember the past are condemned to repeat it") and not repeat mistakes from the past.

So in Chapter 2, I take up the history of the post–World War II social contract by exploring where it came from, what made it last for three decades, why it broke down, and what lessons it offers for the future.

In Chapter 3, I ask what changed in the 1980s, why those changes happened, and why we should care. We should care because the 1980s were a critical turning point in the history of work. The old industrial economy and the institutions, norms, and policies that supported it gradually (and in some cases abruptly) gave way to the emergence of today's global economy driven by knowledge innovation. It was also a time of significant technological innovation—the age of information technology began to take hold in big ways. And finally, it was a time of tremendous transformation in the role of the corporation in America and in labor-management relations. I record those changes in some detail because many (if not most) of them are with us today and will need to constitute starting assumptions as we look to ways of shaping the future of work.

In Chapter 4, I catalog the range of innovations that came out of the crises of the 1980s and in the years since then, up to today. These are the seedbeds of innovation for the future. Many have yet to grow to a scale large enough to have a big impact on the workforce and on society as a whole, yet history tells us that these local innovations might at some point be ready for the national stage.

Then in Chapter 5 I sample some of the innovations unfolding today. Some of these take the form of start-ups that put digital technologies to work in new ways that disrupt old ways of doing business and working. Some of these provide great jobs and some do not. Some are focused on solving important social problems and making a profit and some are committed to all three goals—solving a big problem, making profits, and providing good jobs. So the challenge remains to teach current and next-generation entrepreneurs that they too have choices in how they envision and build their organizations—right from the start.

Chapter 6 pulls all this together by first reporting on the results our students generated in their efforts to negotiate the next-generation social contract. Then I bring together what we have learned from our history, from research to date, and from the voices of the next generation to suggest a narrative and set of actions that, if taken together, could bring the realization of the American Dream within the reach of the next generation.

CHAPTER 2

What Was the Postwar Social Contract, Where Did It Come From, and What Made It Work for Three Decades?

Throughout this book I borrow the concept of a "social contract" first developed by Jean Jacques Rousseau and other philosophers to describe the ideal relationship between citizens and their government to capture what I believe constitutes a social contract at work. By the social contract at work I mean *the mutual expectations and obligations workers, employers, and their communities and societies have regarding work and employment relationships*. In this chapter I bring this concept to life by describing the central feature of the social contract that emerged out of the New Deal labor legislation of the 1930s and took hold after the end of World War II. Figure 1.3 captures the essence of that postwar social contract: Wages and productivity moved upward together from 1945 to about 1980 and in doing so helped expand the American middle class and achieve a sustained era of broadly shared prosperity. Let's now look at how this happened.

In the 1920s, the economy was booming and business was flourishing, but the majority of Americans were left behind. Then the economy fell into crisis of the Great Depression. The Roosevelt administration considered British economist John Maynard Keynes's macroeconomic theory that government needed to spend money to get the economy back on track and tried to pursue it in a half-hearted fashion. It succeeded in stabilizing the economy and helping those most in need by enacting a comprehensive set of policy reforms regarding the labor market and labor relations.

The New Deal labor legislation created unemployment insurance, social security retirement and disability pensions, minimum wages, and the regulation of hours through overtime premiums beyond 40 hours per week. Finally, but perhaps most important for the longer run, it created a labor relations law and policy that enabled workers to join and sustain unions that were capable of bargaining for wages, hours, and working conditions and created a set of policies for resolving labor-management disputes. (See Box 2.1 for a summary.) These achievements laid the foundation for a new social contract for the American economy and workforce. But they were not enough to usher in that new social contract. It took a set of actions on the part of workers, employers, unions, and government policy makers to build on this foundation during and after World War II. The result of the New Deal foundation and the collective actions that built on it was a postwar social contract that worked well for most parties (less well for women and minorities than for men) for three decades—a period that in hindsight looks like a golden era for the American economy.

Box 2.1

The New Deal foundations

Four Pillars of the New Deal Labor Policy	What They Did
Unemployment Insurance	Provided income to unemployed workers for a temporary period of time with the expectation they would either be rehired or find a new job as economic conditions improved
Social Security and Disability Insurance	Provided retirement benefits to employees who had worked a minimum number of years and benefits to workers who become disabled and unable to work
National Labor Relations Act	Protected the right of workers to form independent unions and engage in collective bargaining
Fair Labor Standards Act	Established a national minimum wage and overtime pay requirements for a work week of more than 40 hours

The New Deal

Imagine it is 1930 and you are about to finish school and enter the labor force. What is going through your mind?

You came of age in the roaring 20s when the economy was booming. President Calvin Coolidge told you that the "business of the country is business," and the booming stock market proved his point. But somehow you don't feel so optimistic. Your family shared only a little bit of the growth in the mid-1920s (wages went up about 8 to 10 percent, but the giant portion of the gains went to the top 10 percent of the population). And whatever income gains your family made were quickly wiped out by the events following Black Tuesday in October 1929, the day the stock market crashed. By the end of 1930, real wages for average workers were no higher than they had been a decade earlier. Unemployment was 10 percent and rising rapidly. If your family was part of the 13 percent of the population that lived and worked on a farm, you were in even worse shape: You had steadily lost income throughout the 1920s even in the face of the business boom.

And then came the Great Depression. At its worst, 25 percent of the workforce was unemployed. Homelessness grew to the point that a name was invented to describe the communities of shanties homeless people created with anything they could find: Hoovervilles. The point was clear: President Hoover was doing too little to combat the Depression. Farming families in Texas and Oklahoma who could no longer cope with the combination of the Depression and years of drought began the trek westward toward the promise of a better life in California that John Steinbeck described in *The Grapes of Wrath*. It all looked quite hopeless, and to those who valued our American way of life and political system, it looked quite dangerous. Radical insurrection seemed just around the corner!

Losing a job was disastrous in the 1920s and 1930s. There was no unemployment insurance and no health insurance. Keeping your job likely meant a cut in wages and work hours. One report indicated that by 1933 nine out of ten companies had cut wages, 60 percent of the workforce was working part time, and family income had dropped by 45 percent.[1]

---

[1] "Chapter 5: The Depression," Digital History, http://www.digitalhistory.uh.edu /teachers/lesson_plans/pdfs/unit9_5.pdf, accessed March 15, 2014. For other reviews of wage cuts during the Great Depression, see Leo Wolman, "Wages during

That combination of frustration and desire for change led to political change. After the Republicans had controlled the White House for 10 years, Democrat Franklin D. Roosevelt was elected. He ushered in what would become known as the New Deal.

While Roosevelt didn't come into office with a clear agenda for change, at least one of his advisors did. Frances Perkins famously warned the new president that if he chose her to be his Secretary of Labor she would press for legislation to provide unemployment insurance, a national minimum wage, and a program of retirement insurance and disability insurance (see Box 2.2).

Box 2.2

Frances Perkins's vision and agenda

Roosevelt came right to the point. "I've been thinking things over and I've decided I want you to be Secretary of Labor."

Since the call from his secretary, I had been going over arguments to convince him that he should not appoint me. . . . I said that if I accepted the position of Secretary of Labor I should want to do a great deal. I outlined a program of labor legislation and economic improvement. None of it was radical. It had all been tried in certain states and foreign countries. But I thought that Roosevelt might consider it too ambitious to be undertaken when the United States was deep in depression and unemployment.

In broad terms, I proposed immediate federal aid to the states for direct unemployment relief, an extensive program of public works, a study and an approach to the establishment by federal law of minimum wages, maximum hours, true unemployment and old-age insurance, abolition of child labor, and the creation of a federal employment service.

The program received Roosevelt's hearty endorsement, and he told me he wanted me to carry it out.

Source: Frances Perkins, *The Roosevelt I Knew* (New York: Viking Press, 1946).

---

the Depression," *National Bureau of Economic Research Bulletin* 46 (May 1, 1933): 1–5, http://www.nber.org/chapters/c2256.pdf; and Horst Mendershausen, "Changes in Income Level, 1929–1933," in *Changes in Income Distribution during the Great Depression* (New York: National Bureau of Economic Research, 1946), 12–22, http://www.nber.org/chapters/c5307.pdf.

Where did her ideas come from? She didn't make them up. This brings us to our first lesson that can inform efforts to build a new social contract going forward.

All innovations are local. Most of our federal labor and social legislation was first conceived, incubated, and tested at the state level and/or in private-sector settings.

Frances Perkins knew first-hand that there had been a good deal of experimentation with these programs in progressive states such as Wisconsin, New York (where Perkins had been commissioner of the state department of labor when Roosevelt was governor), and Massachusetts. Many of these programs were first developed by academics from the University of Wisconsin under the tutelage of Professor John R. Commons. He earned the title of "Father of the New Deal," since many of his ideas, carried forward by his students, found their way to Washington in the Roosevelt administration.

Consider, for example, how unemployment insurance and Social Security came into being. This is how historian Arthur Schlesinger Jr. told the story. Shortly after taking office, President Roosevelt gave his secretary of labor, Frances Perkins, the green light to work on the agenda she had laid out for him prior to accepting his offer to become "Madam Secretary," as she was later called. She went to work on the idea of creating an unemployment insurance system by drawing heavily on experts from Wisconsin who had worked with John R. Commons to first propose an "experienced-based" state system in 1921. Commons's students Paul Raushenbush and Elizabeth Brandeis Raushenbush (the daughter of Supreme Court Justice Louis Brandeis), University of Wisconsin professor Edwin Witte, and Arthur Altmeyer developed a plan that called for state-level administration of unemployment insurance funded through a payroll tax that was prorated based on the level of unemployment a firm experienced. After considerable debate over the technical details of this approach, the Roosevelt team adopted it and the president endorsed it.

In parallel, another group tackled the question of how to create an old-age insurance system and some means of providing for the families of workers who died or became permanently disabled. The president had already expressed his views to Madam Secretary on this issue. According to Schlesinger, Roosevelt said to Frances Perkins: "I see no reason why every child, from the day he is born, should not be a member of the social security system. . . . From the cradle to the grave they ought be in a social insurance system." He went on to describe his views on how this insurance system should be financed: "If I have anything to say about it, it will be contributed . . . both on the part of the employer and the employee, on a sound actuarial basis. It means no money out of the Treasury."[2]

The rest is history. In January 1935, Roosevelt's social security and unemployment insurance bill was submitted to Congress. It was hotly debated, often in terms that should sound quite familiar to those who have followed the debates over "Obamacare."

A leading business group, the National Industrial Conference Board (I will return to this group's views on issues later), said: "Unemployment insurance cannot be placed on a sound financial basis. It will facilitate ultimate socialist control of life and industry." Alfred Sloan of General Motors said, "The dangers are manifest." James L. Donnelly of the Illinois Manufacturers' Association insisted that the new bill would undermine the American way of life by "destroying initiative, discouraging thrift, and stifling individual responsibility."[3] Republicans in Congress such as Representative John Taber of New York channeled these views: "Never in the history of the world has any measure been brought in here so insidiously designed as to prevent business recovery, to enslave workers, and to present any possibility of the employers providing work for the people." Representative Daniel A. Reed concurred: "The lash of the dictator will be felt and twenty-five million free American citizens will for the first time submit themselves to a fingerprint test."[4]

---

[2] Arthur M. Schlesinger Jr., *The Age of Roosevelt: The Coming of the New Deal, 1933–1935*, vol. 2 (Boston: Houghton, Mifflin, 1958), p. 308.

[3] Ibid., p. 311.

[4] Ibid.

In the end, after a long debate and a number of amendments, the Social Security Act of 1935 was enacted. It provided unemployment insurance, old-age insurance, and disability insurance programs. Little did these policy makers or their supporters and critics in Congress know that some 50 years later Republicans and Democrats alike would describe Social Security as the "third rail" of politics that was never to be touched.

If this social legislation was controversial, consider the most difficult of all parts of the New Deal to be enacted—legislation to protect workers' rights to join a union and engage in collective bargaining over their wages, hours, and working conditions.

This was not one of the pieces of legislation Roosevelt or his cabinet members initiated or even initially supported. Instead, its chief sponsor was Senator Robert Wagner of New York. The "Wagner Act" (formally the National Labor Relations Act), passed in 1935, shared two similarities with other parts of the New Deal: It built on local-level innovations, in this case in the private-sector clothing, coal, and railroads industries, and it was informed by the work of labor economists and historians who had studied and help guide collective bargaining programs in the era before the New Deal.

The final plank of the New Deal labor legislation, the Fair Labor Standards Act of 1938, instituted the nation's first minimum wage (25 cents per hour), required employers to pay overtime for a work week of more than 44 hours (later lowered to 40 hours), and abolished most child labor. President Roosevelt strongly supported this legislation, which Secretary Perkins and her staff at the Department of Labor had developed. Business strongly opposed it. Labor leaders were lukewarm in their support, fearing in part that government-mandated minimum wages would undermine unions and collective bargaining. Secretary Perkins's staff developed parallel laws that required government contractors and employers in government-financed construction projects to pay "prevailing wages"; these laws were also enacted.[5]

---

[5] See Jonathan Grossman, "Fair Labor Standards Act of 1938: Maximum Struggle for a Minimum Wage," *Monthly Labor Review* (June 1978), http://www.dol.gov/dol/aboutdol/history/flsa1938.htm.

I present this history, focusing particularly on the staff work done at the Department of Labor under a strong and well-informed secretary, to contrast it with the inaction on labor policies in recent Democratic (and Republican) administrations.

> *What can we learn from this experience that would help inform where we need to go? I believe the key lesson to take away from this New Deal history is that if we are to go beyond the divided policies that are always associated with labor legislation in the United States, the following elements must be in place: a strong policy champion, a government department staffed with professionals who can provide deep analysis of labor issues, and access to the expertise created by academics who have helped invent the private and state-level innovations that provide the evidence that proposed policies work.*

The Macro Engine for Growth

Roosevelt did not begin his efforts to cope with the Great Depression with the New Deal legislation. His first and most urgent task upon taking office in 1932 was to stabilize the financial system. He implemented a bank holiday to stop the run on withdrawals. Then he embarked on a spending program to try to regenerate economic growth. By 1937, he had partially succeeded. But then the inflation hawks of his administration won out and took actions to raise interest rates and limit the inflow of gold into the country (our currency was still tied to the value of gold) and the country fell back into recession.[6] It took the military buildup and subsequent wartime production and expansion of the military forces to finally bring unemployment down to pre-Depression levels.[7]

---

[6] Peter Temin and David Vines, *The Leaderless Economy* (Princeton, NJ: Princeton University Press, 2013), p. 56.

[7] Robert J. Gordon and Robert Krenn, "The End of the Great Depression 1939-41: Policy Contributions and Fiscal Multipliers," National Bureau of Economic Research Working Paper 16380, September 2010, http://www.nber.org/papers/w16380.

While the government spent enough in the 1930s to keep the economy from sinking further into decline and to contain the social chaos that threatened to replace our democratic government with a more radical—socialist, Communist, or right-wing totalitarian—alternative, it took the massive expenditures of World War II to finally pull the economy out of recession and get back to something close to full employment. At the same time, the wartime labor shortages (of military-age men) brought in massive female labor force participation. Rosie the Riveter helped produce wartime goods and keep young families afloat while young men—husbands and fathers—went to war.

Again there is a lesson for today.

> *It took massive government spending to recover the jobs that had been lost in the Great Depression. After the war, the restored purchasing power of consumers was able to sustain a strong labor market for years to come.*

While the war buildup brought the unemployment problem under control, a new challenge emerged: How could the government keep wartime production going without work stoppages and without letting inflation get out of control? The answer turned out to be a little-known and underappreciated institution composed of government, business, and labor leaders that was quite effective in the short run and important for creating the principles and practices that would help usher in decades of shared prosperity after the war. The institution was called the National War Labor Board (NWLB).

Government as Innovator: The War Labor Board

Imagine you are a newly minted PhD economist schooled in the latest developments in economic theory who is suddenly called upon to help manage the wartime agencies. You now must put your theoretical knowledge to work on the practical processes of collective bargaining, wage determination, and labor-management relations. Box 2.3 presents a quote from one the best known of these young economists, Clark Kerr, who went on to become one of the nation's leading mediators and arbitrators and eventually the president of the University of California.

Box 2.3

Clark Kerr's story

When I entered the field of industrial relations, I had a chance to practice the art of peaceful solutions. My first experience in the field [while studying for my PhD] was in the fall of 1933 during the bloody cotton pickers' strike in the great Central Valley of California. Then, later[,] . . . from 1940 to 1945 I became the leading arbitrator of industrial disputes in the Seattle region. This led to my participation during World War II in the work of the regional War Labor Board stabilizing wages and settling labor disputes, hundreds of them. After the war, I continued in arbitration and became a leading arbitrator on the West Coast. I saw how violence once unleashed came to lead an uncontrolled life of its own. I saw how patience and reason led to less costly processes and better solutions than did passion and violence.

Source: Clark Kerr, *The Gold and the Blue: A Personal Memoir of the University of California, 1949–1967*, vol. 1, *Academic Triumphs* (Berkeley: University of California Press, 2001), p. 14.

Members of the NWLB such as Clark Kerr and Professor George Taylor from the University of Pennsylvania helped invent and spread many of the employment practices that enabled professional personnel management and collective bargaining to work effectively for decades to come. Rational internal job structures and wage differentials, formulas that adjusted wages for changes in the cost of living, comparisons of wages within industries and occupations, fringe benefits including health insurance and pensions, grievance procedures that included arbitration for resolving day-to-day disputes—all of these grew out of decisions or recommendations of the NWLB. And based on their experiences in their early careers in working with management and labor to apply these new principles, a cadre of young professional labor relations "neutrals" (i.e., individuals who were neither labor nor management representatives but worked with both sides as mediators or arbitrators to resolve their disputes) was created who went on to apply and adapt these practices in industry for decades to come.

The lesson: Creative and knowledgeable "neutrals" can make a difference and invent solutions to practical problems. But they have to understand the nature of labor (and other) market forces and not be captured by the interests of one party or another—in this case business or labor. And, they can't be so tied to past practices that they are not able to invent new solutions for the future.

By far the most important of these innovations involved fringe benefits. The NWLB encouraged bargaining on health insurance and pensions as a way of holding wages in check and keeping labor peace. This is how employers became the providers of long-term economic security and health care coverage, something that worked well for many years for those who were covered. But this legacy is now an albatross around the neck of the economy. I will discuss how to wean ourselves from this legacy in Chapter 6.

The lesson: It made good sense to use employers as the transmission belt for spreading health insurance and pension coverage when large firms and long-term employment with a single firm was the dominant model of employment relations. This is no longer the case, and we now have to wean ourselves from this outmoded approach to funding and transmitting coverage of these key benefits.

The Postwar Economy and Labor Market: Boom or Bust?

Following World War II, many economists worried that the economy would fall back to prewar levels of stagnation as government wartime expenditures declined. In 1943, economist Paul Samuelson, who later was awarded the Nobel Prize in economics, wrote that when the war ended, "some ten million men will be thrown on the labor market" leading to the potential for "the greatest period of unemployment and industrial dislocation which any economy has ever faced."[8] Another future Nobel Prize

---

[8] Paul Samuelson, "Full Employment after the War," in *Postwar Economic Problems*, edited by S. E. Harris (New York: McGraw-Hill, 1943), quoted in Cecil Bohanon,

winner, one of the most famous European economists of the time, Gunner Myrdal, offered the even more dire warning that the economic challenges in Europe would lead to an "epidemic of violence."[9]

But lo and behold, neither Samuelson's nor Myrdal's prediction came to pass. Instead, the postwar period saw the emergence of a robust economy in the United States led by pent-up consumer demand and fueled by international financing that supported the rebuilding of the war-torn societies of Europe and Japan. This was achieved by a combination of the private-sector investment that was needed to help industry transition from military goods back to the production of consumer goods and a supportive set of education and labor market policies and institutions that matched the needs of the postwar economy.

Together, these business investments and institutions created what would become known as the postwar social contract. Here's how it was created and sustained for the three decades following the war.

The Postwar Social Contract

The Role of Education

Let's start with the role education played in helping to build a prospering postwar economy. When World War II ended, 10 million veterans who had put their careers on hold to serve their country returned home to relaunch their family lives and careers. Some, like Ted Williams, the most famous Red Sox player ever, were so talented that they could pick up where they left off. The first year he was back William batted .342, hit 38 home runs, batted in 123 runs, and led the Red Sox to win the American League pennant (but, as all Red Sox fans know, not the World Series; that would have to wait until 2004).

Others were not yet at the top of their game, and the nation worried about what to do with them. Fortunately, national leaders were also worried about the futures of veterans and felt they owed them some

---

"Economic Recovery: Lessons from the Post World War II Period," September 10, 2012, http://mercatus.org/publication/economic-recovery-lessons-post-world-war-ii-period.

[9] Ibid.

assistance. For those who grew up on their family's farm, going back was not a good option since advances in technology—tractors and milking machines, for example—were greatly reducing the need for farm labor and small family farms were becoming more and more tenuous and less likely to survive long enough to be passed on to the next generation. Fortunately, the manufacturing sector beckoned. Large industrial firms were growing and needed middle managers and talented technical engineers. But these opportunities required further education.

The GI Bill was created to meet these needs. By any standard (particularly compared to today!), the benefits were generous. The Servicemen's Readjustment Act of 1944 (the official name of the GI Bill) entitled anyone with 90 days or more of military service to one year of tuition and paid fees for education up to a maximum of $500 per year. This increased for each month of service up to a maximum of 4 years of support. In addition, single veterans received a stipend of $50 a month and married veterans received $75 a month while in school.

About 12 percent of returning veterans took up the opportunity to go to college. One study estimates that the net effects of the GI Bill and military service in World War II increased college graduation rates by between 5 and 8 percent. Although other studies estimate smaller effects, there is no question that the benefits were generous enough to provide a strong incentive for veterans to go to college, support a family sufficiently while the veteran completed a degree, and leave the veteran with little or no debts to repay. These extensive benefits not only encouraged college attendance but very likely helped increase the range of colleges available to many who otherwise would have been limited to lower-cost institutions. As just one example, over 90 percent of those admitted to the Harvard Business School in 1947 were supported by the GI Bill.

During the postwar years, American universities grew in size and stature to become the world's best and most accessible system of higher education. My favorite example of a great public university is the University of Wisconsin. The relatively low cost of college allowed many young people to become the first member of their families to attend and graduate from college, often through a combination of part-time work, scholarships, low-interest loans, and family support. My first semester of tuition at the University of Wisconsin, Manitowoc County Center, a two-year institution that provided transfer credits to the Madison campus, was $105. (In 2013, one semester's tuition at the same institution cost $5,000). If I recall correctly, I earned about $800 to $1,000 in summer jobs and another $500 or so in part-time jobs during the school year. This was more than enough to finance the costs of these years and to put enough aside to cover the cost of living in Madison for the final two years of undergraduate work. Years later I enjoyed telling our youngest son that my wife and I spent more on his preschool education than I spent on my entire college education, right up through the PhD! This would not have been possible without the supports of a low-cost, high-quality state university, scholarships from the state and from the local community, and fellowships from the National Science Foundation and other government agencies.

The quality of this education was unsurpassed. While funding higher education was always controversial in state politics, successive waves of state legislators and governors supported Wisconsin's state university with generous budgets. But this support has decreased markedly since 2005 and reached a nadir (I hope) with the budget cuts Governor Scott Walker imposed after he was elected in 2010. The year I graduated from the university (1973), the state government covered 43 percent of the university's total budget; by 2012, the state's contribution had fallen to 15 percent. Over this same time period, the proportion of the university's income from tuition increased by nearly 50 percent, rising from 11 percent in 1973 to 16 percent in 2012.

I summarize the University of Wisconsin experience to illustrate the risks America is facing as it defunds public universities and makes it harder and harder for young, ambitious, and talented people from families of modest means to use these premier institutions as a channel for upward mobility. Although higher education remains one of the things America excels at, if the nation is to retain this position, significant transformation will be necessary in the years ahead. For this reason, we need to understand the role of education in fostering and supporting the postwar social contract, if only so we can figure out what features need to be retained and reinforced and what features need to be to changed and transformed in the future.

The Role of Collective Bargaining

In the postwar years, demand for production workers was brisk as factories retooled to meet the pent-up demand for consumer goods that had not been available during the war. Unions entered a period of growth and became permanent institutions in the United States, thanks in part to the duty of employers to bargain with unions specified in the 1935 National Labor Relations Act. But workers also had pent-up demands following years of wage controls. As these controls were lifted, numerous strikes broke out. More time was lost to strikes in 1946 than any other year before or after. If any business leaders thought the end of the war would open the door to a return to the preunion conditions of the 1920s, the strike wave and the newfound power of industrial unions demonstrated that this was not an option. Instead, employers needed to come up with a way to stabilize labor relations so they could take advantage of growing markets for American goods at home and abroad. The postwar social contract emerged from this setting.

President Truman hoped that the cooperation between labor and business that had developed during World War II could be carried over to the peacetime economy. In 1945, he called a meeting of national labor and business leaders to discuss the principles of a potential postwar labor-management accord. Although the parties came close to such an agreement, they came up short on one issue: They could not agree on the limits of union influence in management decisions.

Progressive union leaders such as Walter Reuther, president of the United Auto Workers (UAW), envisioned a postwar labor relations system in which workers would contribute to improving operations and help steer businesses to broader social purposes, just as he had led the process of retooling industry in the early 1940s to build tanks and ships to support the war effort. But business leaders strongly opposed having an open-ended agenda for labor-management relations—they wanted to retain management's right to manage businesses.

The lesson: It is likely that there will never be a permanent accord between labor and business. But when the nation is in crisis, both sides can be mobilized to act in the national interest. At least this was the case in the past. What steps might be taken to rally the same sense of national solidarity to help forge a new social contract suited to today's economy and the workforce of the future?

In the absence of a shared vision for the future of labor-management relations in the postwar years, the parties each had to pursue their own strategies. Walter Reuther, who, depending on one's point of view, was either the "most dangerous man in Detroit" or the most progressive labor leader of his time, pursued his vision through bargaining with auto companies. (George Romney, the future governor of Michigan and father of Mitt Romney, the Republican candidate for U.S. president in 2012, is the one who called him "the most dangerous man in Detroit."[10]) Reuther wanted workers to have a voice in management decisions about production, pricing, and product development in addition to the legally prescribed range of bargaining over wages, hours, and working conditions. But management had a different idea, and few of Reuther's labor leader colleagues supported his "socialist"-sounding ideas. Instead, GM's CEO proposed what the editors of *Fortune Magazine* labeled the Treaty of Detroit. In return for labor peace, GM would agree to a wage formula that would link wage increases to growth in productivity and to the cost of living.[11]

How did the wage norms and settlements between GM and the UAW spread across the economy? It is worth reflecting on this question, not just for the historical record but because, as I will discuss later, a big strategic puzzle today is how to make the best practices of leading firms the norm in business. To understand how this happened, we need to introduce an old labor relations term: pattern bargaining.

Pattern bargaining is the process whereby unions seek to spread wage settlements achieved in one firm to competing firms in their industry or labor market in order to take wages out of competition. By doing so, they provide stability in labor relations and gradually raise or ratchet up the floor on wages, benefits, and working conditions. In today's parlance, we might describe this as a way of avoiding a race to the bottom.

---

[10] Nelson Lichtenstein, *The Most Dangerous Man in Detroit: Walter Reuther and the Fate of American Labor* (New York: Basic Books, 1995).

[11] Ibid.

For example, the UAW took the GM agreement to GM's direct competitors, Ford and Chrysler, and was able to get them to agree to the same settlement. Unions in other industries such as steel, electronics, oil and gas, utilities, and rubber likewise sought to match what the auto workers achieved. The net result was the tandem movement in wages and productivity from the mid-1940s through the 1970s that is depicted in Figure 1.3. This how the postwar social contract became the national norm.

Econometric evidence has demonstrated that collective bargaining was a particularly effective way to use pattern bargaining to reduce wage differences within industries. That meant that there was no single national wage pattern. Instead, a norm developed by which unions bargained for wages and employers agreed to wage proposals based on comparisons with the wages of similar-sized competitors in the same industry. This norm was enforced by the bargaining power of unions and was copied by nonunion firms that wanted to remain nonunion. That is how wage increases were spread across competitors within industries and labor markets. The wages of white-collar workers and middle managers also increased as the result of union-negotiated wage increases because personnel managers were careful to maintain reasonable differentials between managers' wages and the wages of the workers they supervised. The salaries of CEOs and top management were held in check for fear that unions would demand equivalent pay increases if they observed those at the top of their companies disproportionately feathering their own nests. This combination of union power and pattern bargaining is how what some refer to as social norms kept wage and income inequality from getting out of hand in the postwar period.

I polled the students in the online class about whether they thought wages and productivity should move together as they did in the heyday of the postwar social contract. An overwhelming majority—83 percent— agreed that they should. They saw it as a sensible general norm or principle for wage setting. But many also worried that this might be difficult to do in the future. Here is a sampling of student comments on this issue.

> The lack of congruence between wages and productivity [in recent decades] is one of the reasons we have such drastic income inequality. If the benefits of all that productivity are not going to

the workers, then they are going to the owners. Thus the owners, i.e., the major stockholders, are becoming enriched at the expense of the workers who are creating the wealth for them.

Shareholders and managers have always been and always will be motivated to increase profits[,] which means paying workers the lowest possible wages. In the post-war era, workers had the power (mostly through unions but government also played a role) to force employers to pay higher wages. Since the 1970s workers have lost that power. To increase wages, workers must regain the power to force wage increases. Wage increases will not happen through employer charity.

The lesson: Norms don't appear out of thin air. Behind every norm lies an idea and the power to enforce and spread that idea.

From Steady State to Atrophy

All these cross-cutting institutions helped support and sustain the social contract from the 1950s through the 1970s. During these years, as the lines in Figure 1.3 indicate, the wage-setting formula initiated by GM and the UAW in the 1940s kept productivity and real wages moving upward roughly in tandem. This is not to say that there were not rough spots along the way. In the 1960s, concerns that wage-price spirals were fueling inflation led the Kennedy and Johnson administrations to introduce wage and price guideposts in an attempt to restrain inflation. In the early 1970s, runaway wage increases in the construction industry that threatened to spread to other industries led the Nixon administration to take even stronger action in the form of wage and price controls. And later in the 1970s a period of "stagflation"—slow economic growth while wages and prices continued to increase—created a crisis that eventually led to dramatic change in both economic policies and political leadership. The postwar social contract had matured but was not adapting to an incrementally changing environment.

Indeed, the 1960s proved to be a tumultuous decade in both employment relations and American society in general. In employment relations, the

1960s began with much concern that advances in technology (referred to at the time as "automation") were gradually but steadily eliminating jobs and creating a population of permanently unemployed workers (called structural unemployment). A host of new policies were implemented to support retraining, geographic relocation, and regional economic development to cope with the consequences of persistent unemployment. The employment and training policies and infrastructure in place today are essentially carryovers from these beginnings of a national labor market policy.

The automation scare proved to be overstated and premature. Just as World War II expenditures brought the labor market out of the Great Depression, expenditures for the Vietnam War in the 1960s did more to bring down the unemployment rate than the new employment and training policies did, helped along by the technological innovations that spawned the growth of the emerging high-tech industries. Once again the lesson is clear:

When an economy needs to create new, high-quality jobs, it must have strong, growth-oriented macroeconomic policies in place and must nurture technological invention, entrepreneurship, and innovations.

But the trauma of the Vietnam War and the civil rights battles of the 1960s began to create schisms in the fabric of the social contract. Coming of age and entering the labor force in the 1960s was a heady experience. Everyone was fighting with everyone. The civil rights movement took off with marches in Selma, protests in Birmingham, and the famous March on Washington, where Martin Luther King Jr. gave his "I Have a Dream" address. The Vietnam War tore the country apart, and student protests at leading universities brought police and the National Guard to campuses across the country, in some cases, as at Kent State, with tragic consequences. Cities such as Los Angeles and Detroit were literally on fire as the result of civil rights riots. Young people became disillusioned with all major institutions—with labor unions for being "hardhats" who supported the war and resisted integration, with businesses for making napalm and other horrific war materials, with university leaders for being part of the establishment. American society seemed to be coming apart.

While college students opposed the war, the most visible leaders of the labor movement and the business community either continued to support it or kept their personal misgivings to themselves. While some labor and business leaders supported civil rights activism, the most visible leaders— particularly the leaders of the AFL-CIO—remained silent or aloof. George Meany, president of the AFL-CIO, chose to be out of town the day of Martin Luther King's March on Washington in 1963, leaving his rival, Walter Reuther, to be the highest-ranking labor leader to march with Rev. King. Young people saw unions as so entrenched a part of the "establishment" that they had little to offer the next generation.

Meanwhile, the world of work was changing below the sight lines of both established labor and management. New ideas for organizing work in more flexible ways had begun to emerge that allowed individuals and teams to flourish and informed how work was done, especially in the new high-technology industries and companies such as Hewlett Packard, Texas Instruments, Digital Equipment Corporation, and, later, Intel, Apple, Dell, and their progeny. These companies used new ideas to organize work, motivate employees, and provide a satisfying and challenging work environment. Labor unions, stuck in organizing models that assumed that workers would be dissatisfied with their jobs and distrusted their bosses, never adapted in ways that convinced workers in these emerging industries that they needed union representation. Gradually, the firms and unions that occupied the high-road cell in Figure 1.1 in the postwar era were migrating in the direction of the low-road cell with high wages but declining profits and competitiveness. As a result, throughout the 1960s and 1970s, union membership began what would turn out to be a long-term decline.

By the mid-1970s, the divide between the unionized sector of the economy that carried forward the wage formulas and work practices of the earlier era and the newer, faster-growing high-tech sectors of the economy was apparent. The difference between union and nonunion wages had increased from about 5 percent to 10 percent in the 1950s and 1960s to an average of 20 percent by the mid-1970s—a differential that caused employers with unionized workforces to cut jobs and to become more and more concerned about their ability to compete. The pressures for significant change were building.

The most visible political warning signal—really a shot across the bow of labor-management relations—came in 1977–1978, during the Carter administration, when a mild form of labor law reform (the Labor Law Reform Act of 1978) that was backed by the labor movement failed in Congress. The business community was emboldened by the experience of blocking this reform in a government led by a Democratic president and Congress. Labor and the Democrats fell one vote short of breaking a Senate filibuster.

Economic warning signs were equally ominous. The stagflation of the 1970s doomed Jimmy Carter. It took the shock of a movie-star president to change the course of history, a history today's next generation is inheriting.

The lesson: Organizations and institutions fall into patterns of behavior that do not automatically or easily adapt to incremental changes in their environment. They are like the mythical frog put in a kettle of water that is heated gradually and doesn't take action to hop out until it is too late. Radical or disruptive change—departures from well-established routines that have worked for a long time—often can only be achieved (or certainly have a higher likelihood of being tried out) in new organizations or institutions.

CHAPTER 3

What Changed in the 1980s and After?

The 1980s will be recorded by economic historians as the decade the postwar social contract broke down. A look back at Figure 1.3 shows this vividly. Wages have flatlined since then. Nothing has yet replaced the broken social contract.

Triggering Events

Three events converged at the beginning of the 1980s that broke the inertia in the labor-management relations of the 1970s.

1. The country replaced Jimmy Carter, a Democrat, with Ronald Reagan, a conservative Republican.
2. The economy fell into a deep recession in large part induced by Paul Volcker, a strong-minded chair of the Federal Reserve Bank who single-handedly took up the task of breaking the back of inflation, even if it meant breaking it on the backs of American workers.
3. International competition hit the auto, steel, and other manufacturing industries of the Rust Belt with a vengeance as the value of the dollar rose relative to the Japanese yen and the Japanese demonstrated that the goods they had to export were of high quality (and in some cases higher quality than their U.S. counterparts) and were produced at higher levels of productivity than could be achieved in the United States.

Together these three forces ushered in an era of managerial militancy in labor relations. President Reagan set the tone by firing air traffic controllers who engaged in an illegal strike in August 1981. Private-sector employers took their cue from the president and became proactive in demanding wage concessions and implementing what came to be called two-tier wage agreements: that is, a lower wage rate for new hires than for existing workers doing the same jobs. One estimate indicated that over 40 percent of collective bargaining agreements that were reached in the early 1980s involved some form of concession in wage settlements.[1] Any relatively new hires in the auto industry today will be able to relate to this fate. They too work alongside their seniors, doing essentially the same work for about 30 percent less pay.

The pattern bargaining era ended. So too did the value of the strike threat as a source of bargaining power for workers. Strikes at the Phelps Dodge copper mines, the Greyhound bus line, and the Hormel meat-packing company ended in deep wage cuts in the 1980s. A strike at Eastern Airlines ended in liquidation of the company. Econometric evidence shows that during this period, the effects of strikes on wages went from positive to negative (from the 1950s through the 1970s, industry strike rates were positively associated with wage increases; after 1980, they had a negative or no effect) and the positive wage effects of intra-industry pattern bargaining also came to an end.[2]

These developments created a great academic debate: Were these just temporary setbacks for labor that reflected the deep recession of the early 1980s? Would things return to normal once the economy recovered? Or was this a turning point that signaled the need for fundamental changes in labor-management relations?

History resolved this debate. There was no rebound in union bargaining power or labor-management relations when the economy recovered in the mid-1980s or when it entered a boom in the mid-1990s. The bargaining power that used to accompany the threat of a strike never returned. Yet no new sources of power came along to replace labor's traditional weapon. The bottom line was that unions and the workers they represented were on the defensive, a trend that in many respects continued until recently. (This last sentence is a teaser. It suggests that something new is afoot in rebuilding bargaining power for workers. Stay tuned for a discussion of this in Chapter 5!)

---

[1] Robert J. Flanagan, "Wage Concessions and Long-Term Union Wage Flexibility," *Brookings Papers on Economic Activity* 1 (1984): 183–216.

[2] Thomas A. Kochan, Harry C. Katz, and Robert B. McKersie, *The Transformation of American Industrial Relations* (New York: Basic Books, 1986).

The lesson: The bargaining power labor used to gain from threatening or actually withholding labor is gone and new sources of power are needed going forward. Simply rebuilding unions as the mirror image of what they were in their twentieth-century glory years will not work.

The good news is the shock waves from this breakdown in the postwar social contract jump-started a good deal of innovation in employment practices, some of which suggest a way forward that could, if spread across the country, help create a new social contract tailored to the realities of today's economy and the needs of the next-generation workforce. So let's look more deeply at what produced these triggering events and ushered in an era of innovations in employment relations, again with an eye toward what we might learn for shaping the future of work.

The place to start has to be with changes in the environment of firms and workers that were unfolding, whether or not they were recognized clearly by those who were shaping workplace practices at the time. Each of the forces mentioned here continue to be with us today and must figure into our own efforts to shape the future of work.

Globalization

The postwar social contract thrived in an era when the American economy was growing steadily and U.S. firms were dominant competitors in most other countries around the world. This changed dramatically in the early 1980s. America went from having a consistent positive balance of trade (in which the dollar value of exports exceeded the dollar value of imports) with other countries to experiencing a persistent trade deficit. Nowhere was this more apparent and impactful than in manufacturing, particularly in the auto and steel industries. In the early 1980s, the value of the U.S. dollar increased significantly relative to other currencies, especially relative to the Japanese yen. This corresponded with a rapid influx of Japanese autos, steel, electronics, and other goods into U.S. markets. Japan had improved the quality of its manufacturing products and the productivity of its manufacturing processes to the point where the "Japanese model" became the benchmark for manufacturing in the 1980s. While the Japanese economy declined in the 1990s, by that point other developing countries with lower labor costs—Korea, Mexico, Indonesia, Malaysia, and most importantly China—became havens for the outsourcing of U.S. manufacturing.

The effect was the loss of about one-third of the nation's manufacturing jobs and strong downward pressures on the wages for any work that could potentially be outsourced to another country. These trends continue today. The implication going forward as we think about the future of work is obvious: Today and in the future we must assume that much of economic activity is global, not just national, in scope. Among other things this means we can no longer compete by trying to equalize wages via pattern bargaining. Instead, American workers and employers have to strive to stay ahead of lower-wage competitors with superior technology, workforce skills, and organizational practices—what we call high-road business and employment strategies.

Technology: "It's People Who Give Wisdom to the Machines"

In the 18th century, it was the British Luddites who took clubs to the mechanical looms that were replacing them. In the 1960s, it was the fear that automation would produce massive permanent unemployment. In the 1980s, futurist Jeremy Rifkin predicted that technology would bring an "end to work." We hear some similar warnings today as the digital economy advances. So while there is no shortage of warnings and predictions that the end of work is near, there is little doubt that advances in information technology (IT) and machine intelligence, perhaps along with advances in the life sciences, will profoundly change the demand for labor in the years ahead and will continue to lead to a decline in jobs that machines can and will do.

But it is important to recognize that technology is a not a deterministic force. If it is used creatively, it can be a complement to work (i.e., a force that supports it) rather than a pure substitute for human labor. The best way to bring this lesson home is to look at the experience General Motors had in coping with automation in the 1980s. This lesson only cost them $50 billion, in 1980s dollars no less! The story goes as follows.

In 1980, NBC aired a documentary called "If Japan Can . . . Why Can't We?" Essentially the program reported on the success of Japanese workers in building higher-quality automobiles with fewer work hours (higher productivity) than their American counterparts. GM decided it would step up to meet this challenge. Its solution: automate operations to get rid of costly UAW labor. It pursued this path with gusto in the 1980s, spending a reported $50 billion to install robots and other forms of advanced automation in select factories. I visited two of their most highly automated factories, one in Wilmington, Delaware, and one in Hamtramck, Michigan. In both plants one could see that the strategy was not working well. There were too many robots standing idle and too many vehicles in the repair bay at the end of the assembly process waiting for something to be fixed before they could be shipped. Two little vignettes pulled from my notes on those plant visits tell the story.

> On a tour of the plant our guide points out with considerable pride a walled-off area he describes as the "$5 million room." Once inside the room we saw two work stations, each with a set of lasers beaming at [car] door panels that had come in from external suppliers for inspection for "dimensionality", i.e., to see if they fit within all specifications. Attached to each laser work station was a computer monitor and an operator. I asked the operator to describe what he was doing.

> "See all the data on my screen. Those numbers tell me whether or not the doors we get from our supplier fit our specifications in all dimensions. This is great stuff. Before we had this technology I used to always get into fights with the guy I talked to at the supplier. I'd say a part wasn't right. He'd say it was ok when it left their shop and off we'd go. Now we have the same numbers and equipment so there's no debating."

> I asked: "If they have the same technology and can produce the numbers and check the quality, why do you need this technology here? Aren't you duplicating what they are doing?"

> His answer: "Yeah. But it's simple: They lie!"

> Then, as we moved on with our tour of the assembly line and watched how these high-tech-tested doors were fitted onto the

cars, I noticed (and our tour guide was considerably embarrassed to see) that the workers had rubber mallets in their hands and were gently pounding the door frames into place. Apparently this traditional "technology" was still needed to fix imperfections in fit that remained despite the high-tech investments and checking!

A short time later, I toured a Japanese assembly plant located in Canada and asked our tour guide how they tested their panels for proper dimensionality.

"We don't do that. We assume the supplier got it right. That's their responsibility. We worked with them at the start until we were confident in their ability."

I asked: "You mean you don't have a $5 million room with lasers?

His answer: "We'll let our competitors have that technology."

These two vignettes explain why, despite its $50 billion investment in new technology, GM remained the high-cost auto manufacturer at the end of the 1980s. Careful studies by MIT students John Krafcik and John Paul MacDuffie have documented that the highest levels of productivity and quality in auto assembly plants worldwide were achieved in plants that carefully integrated workforce training, employee involvement and teamwork, and flexible work systems with investments in new technologies.[3] They embodied the Japanese phrase that it is "workers who give wisdom to the machines."

This finding has now been replicated with respect to investments in information technologies in the service and manufacturing industries. Timothy Bresnahan, Erik Brynjolfsson, and Lorin Hitt studied the effects of investment in IT across industries in the 1990s.[4] Their results showed that the biggest returns to IT were realized in organizations that

---

[3] John Krafcik and John Paul MacDuffie, "Integrating Technology and Human Resources for High Performance Manufacturing: Evidence from the Auto Industry," in *Transforming Organizations*, edited by Thomas Kochan and Michael Useem (New York: Oxford University Press, 1992), pp. 208–226.

[4] Timothy Bresnahan, Erik Brynjolfsson, and Lorin Hitt, "Technology, Organization, and the Demand for Skilled Labor," in *The New Relationship: Human Capital in the American Corporation*, edited by Margaret Blair and Thomas Kochan (Washington, DC: The Brookings Institution), pp. 143–197.

combined these investments with innovations in work processes that complemented the new technology. Adam Litwin found the same results in his study of how different clinics at Kaiser Permanente implemented and used electronic medical records technologies.[5]

> *The lesson: IT or other advanced technologies don't stand alone or apart from the people who will use them. Involving the people who will ultimately use them in the design, deployment, and ongoing use of the technologies and adapting work practices in ways that complement these new systems makes the technologies pay off—for firms as well as for the workforce.*

I will apply and extend this lesson in Chapter 5 when I discuss how to capture the benefits associated with the current wave of innovations in digital and life science technologies.

The Financialization of Corporations and Its Effects[6]

Private sector firms, by definition, have always pursued the goal of profit maximization. But for many years during the heyday of the postwar social contract, this goal competed with other values and was tempered by the power of unions that demanded a share of corporate profits for the workforce. This changed dramatically in the 1980s and has not rebounded since then. I can best tell the story of how and why this changed by looking back on how the pressures on CEOs changed over the course of time from the 1960s to today. Indeed, I will start the story even earlier, with the 1949 graduating class of the Harvard Business School.

---

[5] Adam Seth Litwin, "Technological Change at Work: The Effects of Employee Involvement on the Effectiveness of Health Information Technologies," *Industrial and Labor Relations Review* 64, no. 5 (2011): 863–888.

[6] Many other researchers have written about the financialization of American corporations. See, for example, Sanford M. Jacoby, *The Embedded Corporation: Corporate Governance and Employment Relations in Japan and the United States* (Princeton, NJ: Princeton University Press, 2004); William Lazonick, *Sustainable Prosperity in the New Economy* (Kalamazoo, MI: W. E. Upjohn Institute for Employment Research, 2009); Eileen Appelbaum and Rosemary Batt, *Private Equity at Work: When Wall Street Manages Main Street* (New York: The Russell Sage Foundation, 2014).

The Harvard Business School class of 1949 has been acclaimed for producing an exceptionally large number of leaders who dominated and shaped business norms over the next three decades. Many were first-generation college graduates. The combined experiences of growing up in the Great Depression and serving in World War II appeared to have had profound effects on this cohort of business leaders. Their sense of community and responsibility, perhaps along with the balance of power that came from the strength of the labor movement, led them to see their responsibilities as CEOs as more than maximizing short-term earnings. Box 3.1 profiles one prominent member of the class, Peter McColough, who went on to become the CEO of Xerox Corporation.

Box 3.1

Peter McColough, Harvard '49, Xerox CEO

Peter McColough was the CEO of Xerox Corporation from 1968 to 1982. Perhaps as much as anyone, McColough exemplified the type of leadership that supported and reinforced the postwar social contract. He played an active leadership role in community affairs in Rochester, New York, where the company was headquartered, and in national political and government advisory roles; he built strong and positive relationships with the union that represented Xerox manufacturing workers; he was ahead of other companies in initiating total quality and employee involvement processes in partnership with the union in the early 1980s; and, perhaps most importantly, as early as 1968 he initiated an affirmative action program that made it possible for women and minorities to rise to a wide range of executive leadership positions at Xerox. It is no accident that in 2002, Ann Mulchay was named CEO of Xerox and that in 2009 she was succeeded by Ursula Burns, the first African American female CEO of a Fortune 500 firm.

The foreword to a book written by the former editor of *Forbes Magazine* summarizes the norms that seemed to guide this cohort of business leaders and offers a ringing indictment of the generation of CEOs that succeeded them in the 1980s and after.

As I write, it is midsummer 2002. The business and Wall Street people who are in the news today seem a sorry lot compared with most of the [class of 1949]. When I say "sorry lot," I am not just talking about the Ken Lays, the Bernie Ebbers, the Jack Grubmans [CEOs who went to jail]. I also refer to the dozens of CEOs who destroyed corporate balance sheets during the 1990s and early 2000s. They did so by taking on short-term debt to pay for overpriced acquisitions. They went into debt to buy their shares at exalted prices. They showed an utter disregard for the probabilities by promising an endless string of 15 percent and more annual earnings gains. And when they couldn't produce earnings, many of them claimed that earnings didn't matter; only EBIDTA [earnings before interest, taxes, depreciation, and amortization] matters. Others made their stock options pay off by gutting their corporate payroll, literally making themselves rich off the misfortunes of their colleagues. All this in the name of "maximizing shareholder values." . . .

I don't know precisely when the term maximizing shareholder value came into common usage, but in a way I wish it never had. Too often it means using gimmicks to get your stock up. It is rarely taken to mean building a solid business that adds value for your customers and creates exciting careers for your employees.[7]

Other CEOs coming out of this class echoed this critique of the later generation that followed them.

In the twilight of their lives, members of the class of 1949 were shocked and appalled by the corruption within the executive suites of corporate America—in companies like Enron, WorldCom, and Merrill Lynch. "There has been a diminution of values," said Jim Burke [CEO of Johnson & Johnson]. "Greed is a very serious problem in American business." At Johnson & Johnson Burke had been a leader in developing a strict ethical code to guide the company known as the Credo. "I saw that value system as an asset to the business, not as a constraint, but an asset." Tom Murphy [CEO of ABC], easily one of the most respected businessmen of his generation, found the rapacious behavior rampant

---

[7] James W. Michels, foreword to David Callahan, *Kindred Spirits: Harvard Business School's Extraordinary Class of 1949 and How They Transformed American Business* (New York: Wiley, 2002), pp. 6–7.

among CEOs hard to fathom. "It's sad," he said. "We were never guilty of what corporate America does today. We were oriented toward the stockholders. . . . They've got to put some of these white collar criminals into jail." As many 49ers saw it, the bad behavior in corporate America was not just sad; it was also unnecessary. "Social responsibility—and expanding profitability—are not intrinsically at odds with one another," Roger Sonnabend [CEO of Sonesta Hotels] believed. "Quite the contrary. They are two faces of the same coin."[8]

The managers of the postwar era were conditioned to be concerned about balancing the interests of multiple stakeholders—investors, employees, and communities. Consider the following policy statement from the Business Roundtable, a group comprised of 200 CEOs of leading U.S. companies. As late as 1990 they said:

> Corporations are chartered to serve both their shareholders and society as a whole. The interests of shareholders are primarily measured in terms of economic return over time. The interests of others in society (other stakeholders) are defined by their relationship to the corporation.
>
> The other stakeholders in the corporation are its employees, customers, suppliers, creditors, the communities where the corporation does business, and the society as a whole. The duties and responsibilities of the corporation to the stakeholder are expressed in various laws, regulations, contracts, and custom and practice. . . .
>
> The central corporate governance point to be made about a corporation's stakeholders beyond the shareholders is that they are vital to the long-term successful economic performance of the corporation. Some argue that only the interests of the shareholders should be considered by directors. The thrust of history and law strongly supports the broader view of the directors' responsibility to the corporation or to the long-term interests of its shareholders."[9]

---

[8] Ibid.

[9] The Business Roundtable, *Corporate Governance and American Competitiveness* (New York: The Business Roundtable, 1990), p. 5.

Compare the Business Roundtable's view in 1990 with the statement the same group issued just seven years later:

> In the Business Roundtable's view, the paramount duty of management and of boards of directors is to the corporation's stockholders; the interests of other stakeholders are relevant as a derivative of the duty to stockholders. The notion that the board must somehow balance the interest of the other stakeholders fundamentally misconstrues the role of the directors. It is, moreover, an unworkable notion because it would leave the board with no criterion for resolving conflicts between interests of stockholders and of other stakeholders or among different groups of stakeholders.[10]

Like so many other institutional innovations, this one was the product of a very basic idea. It started with a new mathematical formula that was developed for pricing stock options by three finance professors, Fischer Black and Robert Merton at MIT and Myron Scholes at the University of Chicago.[11] The big effect of this invention (aside from garnering Scholes and Merton the Nobel Prize in economics; Black died before the prize was awarded in 1997) was to make it easier for firms to make stock options a significant part of the compensation package for CEOs.

The usefulness of this formula was reinforced when other scholars, particularly Michael Jensen and William Meckling, began popularizing a "principal-agent" view of the firm and the responsibilities of the CEO.[12] In brief, the argument was that managers had been allowed to develop their own ideas of what firms should do, some of which might not contribute to maximizing shareholder interests. Jensen and Meckling suggested that CEO compensation plans should give priority to

---

[10] The Business Roundtable, *Statement on Corporate Governance* (Washington, DC: The Business Roundtable, 1997), pp. 3–4, http://www.ecgi.org/codes/documents/businessroundtable.pdf.

[11] Fischer Black and Myron Scholes, "The Pricing of Options and Corporate Liabilities," *Journal of Political Economy* 81, no. 3 (1973): 637–654; Robert C. Merton, "Theory of Rational Option Pricing," *Bell Journal of Economics and Management Science* 4, no. 1 (1971): 141–183.

[12] Michael C. Jensen and William H. Meckling, "Theory of the Firm: Managerial Behavior, Agency Costs and Ownership Structure," *Journal of Financial Economics* 3, no. 4 (1976): 305–360.

including stock options or other means of more tightly aligning CEO incentives with shareholder interests. CEOs would then do whatever it took to boost stock prices.

Another rising theory in finance promoted by University of Chicago professor Eugene Fama (who also won the Nobel Prize for his work in 2013) further reinforced the importance of stock prices. He argued that the price of a firm's stock was the best and most efficient indicator of the future value of the firm.[13] Therefore, financial analysts only needed to concentrate on likely movements in this indicator when advising clients about where to invest, and this in turn put more pressure on CEOs to manage in ways that boosted the price of their company's stock.

Along with these theories came new debt instruments—sometimes called junk bonds—that allowed firms to borrow more money and buy companies more easily, even in the face of opposition from managers. The era of hostile takeovers and equity buyouts of firms was thereby launched. Actor Michael Douglas memorialized this development with his famous "Greed Is Good" speech in his depiction of a Wall Street takeover artist in the movie *Wall Street.*

As generous and lucrative stock options were inserted into compensation packages of top-level executives, their interests shifted from promoting stable, growing firms to developing incentives to maximize short-term earnings and stock prices at any cost. Decisions to lay off employees shifted from painful, reluctant actions of last resort to proactive "restructurings" to strengthen current and or future earnings. The social norms regarding layoffs changed.

Consider the story of Stanley Tools, a venerable U.S. manufacturing company known for the high quality and durability of its products. *New York Times* columnist Louis Uchitelle documented how that company slowly abandoned its culture of doing everything possible to avoid laying off workers by using layoffs as a strategy of last resort during business downturns to seeing layoffs as a more proactive or preemptive move to restructure the company in order to realize higher short-term profits. The title of his book tells the story in a nutshell: *The Disposable American.*[14]

---

[13] Eugene F. Fama, "Random Walks in Stock Market Prices," *Financial Analysts Journal* 21, no. 5 (1965): 55–59.

[14] Louis Uchitelle, *The Disposable American* (New York: Alfred Knopf, 2006).

The shift from a view of the firm as an institution that should be accountable to shareholders *and* other stakeholders to a financial model of shareholder value above all else continues to dominate business norms and in many ways business school education today. In later chapters, I will note some businesses that operate differently and some encouraging new efforts to challenge this prevailing view, but it remains a force to be reckoned with if the gains from work are to be more equitably shared across all who help produce them.

Changing Education Requirements

There is no specific marker for when the so-called knowledge-based economy took over from the industrial economy, but the 1980s would be as good a marker as any other. The early high-tech firms (IBM, Texas Instruments, Apple, Digital Equipment, Intel, etc.) were all in rapid growth mode and were competing for newly minted graduates with computer-programming and related skills. As I will discuss more fully in the next chapter, manufacturing industries were restructuring operations to drive productivity and improve product quality, and this too required workers who were able to provide ideas for continuous improvement, perform basic statistical charting and analysis, work effectively and solve problems in teams, and in some case program computer-driven machine and/or design tools.

Other evidence that knowledge became more important in the 1980s can be seen in the earning power of college graduates. It grew dramatically over the course of the decade, a trend that has continued since then, although at a somewhat lower rate. Claudia Goldin and Lawrence Katz, two colleagues at Harvard who have tracked these trends over many years, report that U.S. census data showing the wage differential between college and high school graduates was 39 percent in 1980, 54 percent in 1990, and 61 percent in 2000.[15] David Autor at MIT explored this issue further and shows that even accounting for the increased cost of a college education, a college degree still pays positive returns in lifetime earnings. In 1980, the value of getting a college

---

[15] Claudia Goldin and Lawrence F. Katz, *The Race between Education and Technology* (Cambridge, MA: Harvard University Press, 2008), p. 96.

degree compared to a high school degree was $261,000 for men and $138,000 for women; in 2008, these numbers had grown to $590,000 for men and $370,000 for women.

Regardless of whether or not we want to mark the 1980s as the birth of the knowledge economy, these numbers bring home a key point that I will stress repeatedly as I discuss how to shape the future of work: Education, education, education! That is, a good solid advanced (post–high school) education that mixes technical and behavioral skills (communications, problem solving, negotiations, teamwork, etc.) is a necessary foundation for competing in today and tomorrow's job markets. While increased education and skills will not solve the labor market challenges or end inequality as we know it today, having the education and skills needed to identify ways to innovate, more fully develop and use advanced technologies, and improve productivity and quality are critical to the economy, to individuals and families, and to meeting the needs of employers who want to compete on the basis of high productivity and high wages, what I call high-road strategies.

In summary, I focus on changes in the 1980s not just as a historical lesson but as a guide to today and tomorrow's world of work. That pivotal decade served as a wake-up call to many employers, workers, unions, and academics studying work and employment relations at the time. Those paying attention realized that the postwar social contract was broken and would not come back in its same form. The gulf between productivity and wages began to grow during that decade and remains a conundrum today. The shift in bargaining power from workers to employers started then and continues to today. The emphasis on maximizing short-term shareholder values took off in that decade and continues to dominate how finance is taught in business schools and corporate practice. Information technologies (relabeled today as digital technologies) began to spread and eventually demonstrated their potential to enhance productivity when matched with complementary workforce capabilities and organizational practices.

So as we explore in the chapters that follow the innovations these abrupt changes generated in the 1980s and after, let's do so with a mindset that they hold lessons for the future. The 1980s and the decades since may have provided a number of clues to how we can regain control over these forces and shape the future of work. Let's take a look at these clues.

CHAPTER 4

Out of Crisis, Innovation: Seedbeds for the Future of Work

Born of Crisis: An Era of Experimentation and Innovation

Some labor leaders and their management counterparts in highly unionized firms could see that things had changed in the early 1980s and began searching for new directions in labor-management relations. For example, progressive labor leaders such as UAW vice-president Don Ephlin and his corporate counterpart at GM, Al Warren, fostered a series of innovations that laid the foundation for the spread of new work systems. Their two boldest experiments were to negotiate a joint venture with Toyota called New United Motors Manufacturing, Inc (NUMMI)[1] and to create a new autonomous division of GM called the Saturn Corporation. The goal was to make both NUMMI and Saturn learning laboratories for GM, the UAW, and other business and labor leaders. Telling the Saturn story may be the best way to convey the debates of

---

[1] The story of NUMMI is best told in John Krafcik, "Triumph of a Lean Production System," *Sloan Management Review* 30, no. 1 (1988): 41–52; Paul Adler, "The Learning Bureaucracy," in *Research in Organizational Behavior*, edited by Barry M. Staw and Larry L. Cummings (Greenwich, CT: JAI Press, 1992); and Wilhelm Wilms, Alan J. Hardcastle, and Deone M. Zell, "Cultural Transformation at NUMMI," *Sloan Management Review* 36, no. 1 (1994); 99–113. The July 17, 2015, episode of NPR's program *This American Life* also provided information about NUMMI's history: http://www.thisamericanlife.org/radio-archives/episode/561/nummi-2015.

the day and their vision for the future of work, business, and labor management relations.[2]

The Rise and Fall of Saturn

If you drive through the hills of middle Tennessee on I-65 about 40 miles south of Nashville, you'll encounter an exit for the Saturn Parkway. And if you venture to see where it goes, eventually a large industrial complex will appear at another exit for the Donald F. Ephlin Parkway. You will have arrived at the old Saturn Corporation location—a historical landmark of what was supposed to be the test site for a new model of labor-management relations for GM and perhaps for the nation. Our MIT industrial relations research group worked closely with the UAW and with major auto companies before, during, and after Saturn's creation and years of operation. This story is based on our research and personal experiences with the key players who drove and opposed these innovations.[3]

The Saturn story starts with Irving Bluestone, Don Ephlin's predecessor and mentor in the UAW. Bluestone was among the first of America's labor leaders to embrace the idea that frontline workers should have a voice in improving quality and productivity and the way they do their jobs. He initiated what came to be called Quality of Work Life experiments in a number of General Motors plants in the 1970s and negotiated with his GM counterpart to insert language that included these experiments in the UAW-GM national collective bargaining agreement in 1979. When Ephlin, Bluestone's second in command, became the head of the Ford Motor division of the UAW, he carried this idea with him. That shift came just in time, because in 1982 Ford was having a near-death

[2] If you prefer to see a video summarizing the history of Saturn rather than reading through this text, check out excerpts from *What Happened to Saturn?*, Merrimac Films, 2008. You can find it at https://www.youtube.com/watch?v=_Vg_nhgs29w.

[3] For our work on Saturn, see Saul Rubinstein and Thomas Kochan, *Learning from Saturn: A Look at the Boldest Experiment in Corporate Governance and Employee Relations* (Ithaca, NY: Cornell University/ILR Press, 2001). See also Harry C. Katz, *Shifting Gears* (Cambridge, MA: MIT Press, 1984). For another study of Saturn, see Barry Bluestone and Irving Bluestone, *Negotiating the Future: A Labor Perspective on American Business* (New York: Basic Books, 1992).

experience and its UAW contract was up for renegotiation. Ephlin and his Ford management counterparts Peter Pestillo and Ernie Savoy reached a landmark agreement that many believe saved Ford from bankruptcy and put it on a course toward making quality Job 1 and making labor-management collaboration a feature that decades later would keep the company from requiring a government bailout to stay alive.[4]

The agreement called for employee and union engagement in quality and productivity improvements, new investments in a jointly run union-management training program, and guarantees of employment security through a period of restructuring and staff reductions.

In 1983, Don Ephlin lost his bid for the presidency of the UAW by one vote on the union's executive board. The outgoing UAW president, Doug Fraser, later confided to me that the worst mistake he ever made was to not find that one additional vote for Don. If he had, the future of the union and indeed the future of the American auto industry would have been very different. It might just have avoided the downward spiral that ended in bankruptcy and bailouts for GM and Chrysler.

But now back to Saturn. The consolation prize for losing the election bid was that Don would take over the UAW's GM division. No sooner had he done so than another crisis ensued: GM told him it could not produce small cars competitively using UAW workers in the United States and would have to outsource all future small car models to some lower-cost country.

Don's response was to say, "Let's see if we can do the job." He and his GM counterpart created a Committee of 99 composed of engineers, accountants, mechanics, assembly-line workers, and other specialists to study the world's best practices in work systems, labor relations, and corporate strategies and structures. The result was a decision to create Saturn as "a new kind of company and a new kind of car."

In the Committee of 99's proposal, Saturn would create a union-management partnership from the bottom to the top of the organization. Gone would be the detailed job classifications and complex work rules that

---

[4] See Joel Cutcher-Gershenfeld, Dan Brooks, and Marty Mulloy, *Valuing Work: Principles Driving the Ford-UAW Transformation* (Cambridge, MA: MIT Press, 2014).

dominated traditional plants. Instead, the Saturn labor agreement would be only 28 pages long. UAW wages and benefits would be achieved, but in a different way: workers' pay packets would be a combination of standard wages, production bonuses, and profit sharing. Workers would assemble cars in teams jointly led by UAW and management representatives and the UAW would have co-management responsibilities across all management functions from manufacturing to sales to product development and from the shop floor to the CEO's office.

This radical departure from UAW and GM management traditions was hotly debated, both within these organizations and across the country. But its critics were silenced early on when Saturn was well received by its customers. It achieved the highest quality and customer satisfaction ratings of any American-made automobile. Only Lexus and Infiniti, luxury vehicles that cost twice as much as a Saturn, received higher customer ratings.

But the resentment of traditionalists within both the UAW and GM led to Saturn's downfall. First, they cut back on the investment dollars that had been built into the original business plan for scaling Saturn up to the level needed to be sustainable and profitable for the long run. Then they debated for over three years about whether to approve funding for second-generation models as the initial ones approached the end of their product cycle. By this time, the president of the UAW was Steve Yokich, a union traditionalist who opposed the ideas of employee participation and collaboration with management that his predecessors Bluestone and Ephlin had championed. As a result, Saturn's sales began a long slide downward. (See Box 4.1 for vignettes that further illustrate why Saturn was doomed.) By the time Saturn's product line was finally refreshed with a popular and high-quality SUV and a new but less-well-received sedan, the die was cast. Employee morale at Saturn had plummeted along with productivity. Basic math ruled: If you maintain employment security when demand for your product declines, average cost per product goes up and profits turn to losses.

Internal leadership rivalries erupted and Saturn lingered on life support until GM gave up and closed it down as part of its restructuring during the government bailout process in 2008.

Box 4.1

The leaders who doomed Saturn

Three vignettes from my own experience illustrate the lack of interest in or understanding of Saturn by GM and UAW leaders that contributed to Saturn's downfall:

1. When my coauthor Saul Rubinstein and I finally got an "audience" with GM CEO Richard Wagoner to get his views on Saturn, we were astounded to learn how little he knew about how Saturn worked. We asked him, for example, "What do you think about having UAW representatives as co-leaders of the work teams at Saturn?" his answer was "Really, is that what they do there?" We were on the one hand amazed and on the other startled to learn how little he knew about the organization he was abandoning.

2. When we briefed several GM executives on the results of our work at Saturn in preparation for sharing the results with a larger group of GM managers, one executive said: "Can you just not tell them these results come from Saturn? They will close their ears to anything that comes from there. The reality is that people at Ford have learned more from Saturn than we have."

3. In 1995, while sharing a ride to the airport from a meeting in Washington with UAW president Steve Yokich, I got an earful about why he would never let GM allocate another nickel to Saturn. Among his other comments was that "it's not the f____ kind of union I come from and not the kind we want associated with the UAW." The rest is history. The membership of the UAW was once 1.5 million; now it is down to 390,000.

Mike Bennett, the leader of the UAW local union in the early years of Saturn, discussed with our online students the lessons he took away from his experience. In response to a student's request for his advice for the organization and jobs of the future, he wrote:

"Saturnize America" is my short answer to this broad and important question. Without profit there is no capability for "good" salaries, or "job security." . . . I would focus on hiring responsible people who want to grow, contribute and achieve individual and corporate success with customer focus. Exceed the customers' expectations! Develop a mission statement that every employee has input into, adopt a set of values that are lived up to, be fair and honest with everyone, treat everyone with respect and dignity, insist that everyone be valued-added to the mission and product. Invest in training people and expanding everyone's skill sets, [lead] by example, be a resource to the workers on the plant floor, practice active listening, . . . empower people with decision-making and hold them accountable.

As for the future of jobs? In a global economy the rules have changed. Capital and technology have no borders and no national interests. . . . There is no job or income security without customers and there are no customers without customer focus! Always remember in today['s] global economy, nothing is permanent.

Saturn and NUMMI were by no means the only innovators, and they influenced other union and management leaders to be similarly innovative. Across almost all industries, from steel to telecommunications to airlines, similar smaller-scale innovations in worker participation and labor-management collaboration played out in the 1980s and 1990s. Crisis did indeed spur innovation. Some of these innovations endure today. The most notable and largest in scale, impact, and durability is an ambitious labor and management partnership between the health care giant Kaiser Permanente and the coalition of unions representing the majority of Kaiser employees (see Box 4.2).[5]

---

[5] Thomas Kochan, Adrienne Eaton, Robert McKersie, and Paul Adler, *Healing Together: The Labor-Management Partnership at Kaiser Permanente* (Ithaca, NY: Cornell University/ILR Press, 2009).

Box 4.2

The Kaiser Permanente labor-management partnership

In 1997 the CEO of Kaiser Permanente (KP), the president of the AFL-CIO, and leaders of the coalition of the unions representing employees at KP created what was to become the largest, most long-standing, and most innovative labor-management partnership in the nation's history.

Over its first decade, the partnership helped turn around Kaiser Permanente's financial performance, built and sustained a record of labor peace, and demonstrated the value of using interest-based processes to negotiate national labor agreements and to resolve problems on a day-to-day basis. Among its most significant achievements included negotiation of a system-wide employment and income security agreement for managing through organizational restructurings. This agreement provided the framework to support the introduction of electronic medical records technology on a scale that has made Kaiser Permanente a national leader in this area. In 2005 negotiations, the parties committed to bringing partnership principles more fully to bear on the front lines through use of "unit-based teams" (UBTs) to support continuous improvement in health care delivery and performance.

In the past five years the parties have achieved significant progress in integrating the partnership into the standard operating model for delivering health care by expanding UBTs throughout the organization and demonstrating that high-performing teams that engage employees contribute significantly to improving health care quality and service, reducing workplace injuries, improving attendance rates, and achieving high levels of employee satisfaction with KP as a place to work and a place to get health care. As a result, Kaiser Permanente is now one of the nation's leaders in use of front line teams to improve health care delivery.

Source: Thomas Kochan, "The Kaiser Permanente Labor Management Partnership: 2009-2013," http://mitsloan.mit.edu/group/template/docs/iwer/FINAL-KP report130947.pdf.

But these innovative examples did not spread across other industries and have had a hard time surviving for two key reasons. First, labor leaders couldn't make up their minds on whether to support and champion the new approach or stay committed to the twentieth-century model that has led to their downfall. I participated in two top-level AFL-CIO "Future of Work" study groups and in a Clinton administration Commission on the Future of Worker Management Relations and watched in dismay as advocates for promoting new ideas, including Tom Donahue, secretary-treasurer of the AFL-CIO, and Lynn Williams, president of the United Steelworkers, were unable to convince enough of the traditionalist leaders to chart a new direction. Instead, the labor movement remained ambivalent—not opposed to collaborative methods if a leader wanted to pursue this option but not willing to get out in front and champion a new approach for all workers and their unions.

This is a lesson for the future: Workers need labor organizations that are unambiguous champions for innovation. Ambivalence or institutional inertia will lead to further union decline and alienation of young workers and the public. Experiments with totally new models like the one that developed at Saturn can demonstrate and test new approaches. The key, however, is to learn from new models and then devise ways to support and spread them across the workforce.

The same ambivalence and internal divisions are present in management circles. While scores of management books encourage executives to support human resources as their most important asset, this has not kept firms from holding down wages, cutting benefits, and resorting to layoffs as ways to boost a company's bottom-line numbers. Not surprisingly, in the absence of a shared consensus on a new approach, traditional cost-control employee relations have continued to dominate. Organizations such as Kaiser Permanente are still the exceptional cases.

But the seeds of an alternative business and labor model were planted through these experiments, just as local and state government experimentation planted the seeds for innovations that became national policies in the New Deal legislation in the 1930s. Out of Saturn came the Kaiser

Permanente Labor Management Partnership. Out of Quality of Work Life groups and work teams came the high-performance work systems I will discuss in more detail below.

High-Road and Low-Road Strategies and the Birth of High-Performance Work Systems

Southwest Airlines is in many ways an anomaly in the U.S. airline industry. It has been the most profitable airline in the United States over the past 30 years. Yet:

- Southwest has been roundly and consistently criticized by Wall Street analysts for being too conservative in its growth strategy, too reliant on retained earnings for growth, and too good to its employees.
- Southwest is the most highly unionized air carrier in the country.
- Southwest has continued to do well after the retirement of its high-profile charismatic CEO and founder, Herb Kelleher.
- Southwest Airlines has the highest productivity per employee, is consistently rated as one of the best places in America to work, and rates at or near the top of the industry in quality performance and customer satisfaction.
- Southwest Airlines seldom participates in airline industry conferences and learning consortia, and few of the long-established airlines view Southwest as a model they might learn from and imitate.

This list breaks many stereotypes and combines features that would surprise many: the airline is profitable but is not loved by Wall Street; it is highly unionized but is the most productive airline and the one with the most satisfied and committed workforce; its high performance has been documented but the company is not a laboratory for learning in the eyes of its competitors.[6]

---

[6] Jody Hoffer Gittell, *The Southwest Airlines Way* (New York: McGraw Hill, 2003).

Within almost all industries we can observe at least one and often a number of Southwest equivalents—firms that are driven by values other than the quest for short-term stock prices, have business strategies that stress great customer service and figure out how to deliver this efficiently, and have employees who identify with the company mission and work together to execute the business strategy consistently and effectively and offer ideas for improving performance on a continuous basis. Some of these are highly unionized, some are partially unionized, and some have no unions. Some are relatively early-stage startups with strong, charismatic founders and some are mature organizations that have had multiple CEOs. Some have done well for a long time and then have fallen from grace for one reason or another, and some have been resurrected from the bottom of their industry. Box 4.3 summarizes an op-ed piece I wrote about Market Basket, the example mentioned in Chapter 1 in which employees fought a successful battle to retain this business model and the CEO who fostered it.

Box 4.3

The Market Basket story

Imagine high-level executives, store managers, clerks, and warehouse workers standing outside their stores side by side for a month demanding their CEO be reinstated and the business model that made the company thrive be maintained. And imagine their customer base cheering them while they had to shop elsewhere at considerable inconvenience and expense.

That is exactly what happened this summer at Market Basket, a highly successful New England family owned grocery chain with 71 stores and 25,000 employees. It is clearly the biggest labor story of the year and, if it emboldens others to speak out for similar workplace causes, it may turn out to be the most important workplace event to come along so far in this century.

This broad-based revolt (aka strike) defied all traditional doctrines in labor-management relations, labor law, and corporate governance. It was the outgrowth of a long-standing feud within the owners, the Demoulas family, in which two cousins (Arthur T. and Arthur S.) vied for control of the business.

For years, Arthur T. had led Market Basket to high profits with a business model that provided consumers with low prices and good-quality service by building a highly productive, well-paid, and loyal workforce. But when Arthur S. gained control in June, he fired Arthur T., replaced him with new co-CEOs of his choosing, and began pursuing options to increase the flow of cash to family owners.

Employees demanded that Arthur T. be reinstated and that the business model they built together be restored. They organized rallies that attracted as many as 10,000 workers, customers, and community supporters. They used a "Save Market Basket" Facebook page to spread their message and maintain solidarity across the ranks. At one point, 68 of the 71 store managers signed a statement saying they would not work for anyone but Arthur T. Customers offered countless testimonials about the low prices and good service they were missing and documented the increased costs they incurred in shopping elsewhere by taping their sales receipts to the windows of their local Market Basket stores.

Unlike so many recent labor battles, this one ended happily. After weeks of negotiations, with a strong push for agreement by governors Deval Patrick of Massachusetts and Maggie Hassan of New Hampshire, the board of directors agreed to sell the company to Arthur T. and allow him to lead employees back to work and customers back to their beloved stores.

While these dynamics alone make for an interesting story, there are larger lessons to learn from this case that will be debated in boardrooms, business school classes, labor union halls, social media, and (hopefully) public policy circles.

The broad base of community support that developed for these courageous employees suggests that many could relate to the causes they fought for—a boss who cares for and treats employees with respect, a business model they can be proud of and use to build bonds with customers, and a fair distribution of the profits they help generate. The social media conversations the case sparked suggest that many others are looking for their own ways to speak out and perhaps mobilize against unfairness, inequality, and greedy bosses or owners and to support leaders who buck these trends.

Business executives should take note that American workers and the American public are fed up with owners and shareholders who try to maximize their short-term gains at the expense of employees and customers. Executives are now on notice that in today's transparent world, questions of business strategies and governance are no longer off limits to employees.

Labor union leaders can take heart in the solidarity observed across this broad coalition and ask how they might build and support similar employee-manager-consumer coalitions seeking a fair share of profits, fair prices, and economic growth.

Policy makers should use this case to review our outmoded labor laws, which provided no established avenues for these employees to express their concerns and left the supervisory and managerial employees completely vulnerable to being fired for standing up for what they believed in. It is time to recognize that the old manager-labor divide no longer makes sense and the ossified doctrines of a labor law passed in 1935 needs a comprehensive update.

Business schools had better revise their curriculums to catch up with the workforce. These employees did more to teach everyone about how to run a business that works for owners, employees, customers, and community than any business-school case yet written. It is time to build this knowledge into economics, finance, strategy, operations, and human resource courses so that these skills will become part of the standard toolkit of the next generation of business leaders.

So thank you, Market Basket, for providing the best labor lesson of this century to date. Let's hope others will provide more of the same.

Source: Thomas A. Kochan, "What the Market Basket Deal Says about American Workers," Fortune.com, August 28, 2014, http://fortune.com/2014/08/28/what-the-market-basket-deal-says-about-american-workers/.

The point is that there are alternatives to being a slave to a company's stock price that seem to work well for multiple stakeholders, including long-term investors. Let's see what we have learned about what firms that practice these alternatives seem to have in common. It turns out that answering this question has been a favorite research topic of many of us at MIT and among human resource and labor relations researchers around the country for the past three decades. We think we've learned some things that might well inform us about how to shape the future.

High-Performance Organizational Models

The search for an understanding of what these firms have in common started in the 1980s, when researchers noticed that firms seemed to be going in divergent directions in terms of business strategies and employee relations and were getting fairly predictable different results. The language that was used to differentiate these two approaches quickly evolved to a comparison of "high-road" and "high-performance work systems," which viewed labor as an asset, versus "low-road," "command and control" systems, which viewed labor as a cost like any other factor of production.

A comparison of the business strategies of two household names, Walmart and Costco, illustrates the differences between low-road and high-road business strategies. Walmart has been extremely successful (when judged solely on the grounds of finances and shareholder value) by pursuing a business strategy best captured by its marketing tag line: "Everyday low prices." To achieve this strategy, it places top priority on minimizing and tightly controlling labor costs, discouraging long-term tenure of its "associates," investing little in training and development, and avoiding unions at all costs. Costco's business strategy places a higher value on product quality and customer service, and to achieve these objectives it pays higher wages, invests more in training its workforce to understand and serve customer needs, and has longer tenure patterns (and thus lower turnover costs). As a result, Costco's employees are more productive, stay with the firm longer, and have more discretion to use their time and knowledge to solve customer problems.[7] Both Costco and Walmart are successful on financial grounds. Indeed, between 2010

---

[7] Wayne Cascio, "Decency Means More than 'Always Low Prices': A Comparison of Costco to Wal-Mart's Sam's Club," *Academy of Management Perspectives* (August 2006): 25–28. For more on Costco, Walmart, and the practices of other retail firms, see Zeynep Ton, *The Good Jobs Strategy: How the Smartest Companies Invest in Their Employees to Lower Costs and Boost Profits* (New York: Houghton Mifflin, 2014).

and 2015, Costco's stock price increased 160 percent compared to Walmart's increase of 60 percent.[8] But the biggest difference between the two lies in worker experience and outcomes—Costco workers are better paid, better trained, and stay longer with the company. Some have chosen to unionize and some have not.

What, then, seems to determine the choice of different business strategies? Here is where values and assumptions—mental models, to use a modern term—matter. Way back in 1960, MIT Sloan School professor Douglas McGregor published perhaps the most famous management book of that era, *The Human Side of the Enterprise*. McGregor differentiated between two different mental models management might bring to thinking about its workforce. A Theory X view is that workers are self-interested, uninformed, and uninterested in the enterprise's goals and need to be told how to do their jobs and closely monitored and controlled to make sure they do what needs to be done. An alternative Theory Y mental model is that workers are motivated to do a good job and want to contribute to an enterprise they can be proud to work for and have the knowledge, skills, and motivation to perform well without tight monitoring and controls.

McGregor's key insight was that these mental models become self-fulfilling. Acting on Theory X assumptions breeds resistance and the need for tight controls. Acting on Theory Y assumptions builds trust and correlated behaviors. So values, assumptions, or mental models are a starting point for understanding what makes a high-road and high-performance organization tick.

Then one has to ask the tough question: Assume I have a Theory Y mentality. Can I make it economically viable in my industry? What do I have to do? This is where one often has to push a rock up a hill. The standard economics answer is to do what other firms are doing because those that are surviving and performing well must be managing in the one best, rational way. And the more important labor costs are as a proportion of total costs of goods or services, the more pressure there is on management to control them with whatever it takes. If there are key strategic or core competencies that are critical to achieving high performance, build

[8] "Wal-Mart Stores, Inc. Stock Comparison," NASDAQ.com, http://www.nasdaq .com/symbol/wmt/stock-comparison.

your organization around attracting and retaining people that have these skills and outsource as much other labor as possible to avoid having to pay a premium for less essential work.

Overcoming these tough challenges to a Theory Y value set requires a *system* of mutually reinforcing employment practices. There is no single silver bullet such as a magical incentive compensation plan that will get the needed results. Instead, research has shown a bundle of generic practices exists that needs to be fit to the specific industry and occupational setting.

While the specific practices vary across industries, the generic features include the following:

- Careful selection for employees with strong technical, problem-solving, and collaborative skills
- Significant investment in training and development
- Commitment to building trust and to drawing on employees' knowledge to solve problems, coordinate operations, and drive innovations
- Compensation systems that align employee and firm interests
- Labor-management partnerships in settings where employees are represented by a union and/or professional association

Two decades of research on high-road companies that employ these practices has documented their ability to achieve world-class productivity and service quality in a diverse group of industries, including steel, autos, airlines, telecommunications, apparel, health care, computers, and semiconductors.[9] More recent case studies are now documenting the same patterns of success in smaller firms across manufacturing, retail, and health care establishments.[10]

---

[9] Eileen Appelbaum, Jody Hoffer Gittell, and Carrie Leana, "High Performance Work Practices and Sustainable Economic Growth," Employment Policy Research Network, March 20, 2011, http://www.isn.ethz.ch/Digital-Library/Publications /Detail/?ots591=0c54e3b3-1e9c-be1e-2c24-a6a8c7060233&lng=en&id=128703.

[10] The Hitachi Foundation tracks and supports a number of these cases. See their web page about their Good Companies @ Work program at http://www.hitachi foundation.org/our-work/good-companies-at-work.

This suggests that organizations that function well for both employees and owners, generate good financial and customer service results, and provide good jobs and good career opportunities can come in a variety of industries. What they share appears to be a systemic combination of features: a mission that incorporates the values and strategies of top executives, a commitment to distributing leadership across levels and functions, nurturance of a shared culture across the organization that is aligned with the values of management and employees, cultivation of teamwork, and a desire to empower well-trained and talented frontline workers. My colleague Zeynep Ton brings this point home clearly and concisely in the introduction to her study of high-performance companies in the retail industry.

> There are different ways to make money, I tell my students on the first day of the class I teach on operations for service industries. You can certainly succeed at the expense of your employees by offering bad jobs—jobs that pay low wages, provide scant benefits and erratic work schedules, and are designed in a way that makes it hard for employees to perform well or find meaning and dignity in their work. You can even succeed at the expense of your customers; for example, by offering shoddy service. . . . Many people in the business world assume that bad jobs are necessary to keep costs down and prices low. But I give this approach a name—the bad jobs strategy—to emphasize that it is not a necessity, it is a choice. There are companies in business today that have made a different choice, which I call the good jobs strategy. . . . These companies—despite spending much more on labor than their competitors do in order to have a well-paid, well-trained, well-motivated workforce—enjoy great success.[11]

Students in the online course had a lot to say, mostly based on personal experiences, about the differences of working for high-road versus low-road employers across a wide range of low-wage and high-wage jobs and industries. Here's a sampling:

---

[11] Zeynep Ton, *The Good Jobs Strategy*, p. vii.

My first work experience was at a low road employer (a multinational group of hotels) where employees were paid poorly but were expected to live the so-called brand values. A culture of employer loyalty simply cannot last in such an environment, leading to a very high attrition rate.

When I worked for "low" road employers I was anxious, stressed, and miserable. One person would quit every 2 months, but more people were NOT hired to replace the empty positions.

I currently work at a big hospital. They provided me with complete training, with compensation and benefits. I have the ability to continue my training and education at their expense or with their assistance.

I have a feeling that my "high road" perception of my fast food management job might be slighted skewed but I will stand by it. If it was not company-wide, at least it was true in MY store. All of the employees in my store were treated well, [and had] continuous training, regular but small raises, and opportunities for advancement.

Employers who take the high road invest in training and developing their employees. During my time at this start-up, I had a mentor by my side and I went through extensive training to learn the computer systems which the company used and to familiarize the ways the company operates. I felt I was valued because employees at the company invested their time to help make sure I understood my work.

Students also indicated they are ready to vote with their feet by accepting jobs with organizations that foster high-road strategies and work practices and rejecting jobs with those that do not. I saw this in a class exercise aimed at developing a "Good Jobs" app through interviews with employees of organizations of potential interest to the students. The survey asked employees of these companies a range of questions about their company's business strategies and employment practices. I got a wide distribution of answers to the questions—to the point where 55 percent of the students indicated they would accept a job if offered to them in the company interviewed. But 45 percent would not. Analysis of the data showed that the employers that had in place high-road strategies and practices that research shows predicts both good business performance and good working conditions and employee satisfaction had a much better chance of attracting these potential employees. Using these indicators, we could predict with 80 percent accuracy whether or not these potential employees would accept a job offer. We have a lot more work to do with this instrument before we will be confident of its validity and generalizability, so stay tuned for more work on this issue. But we hope that apps like this one or others such as Glassdoor[12] or Indeed[13] that provide similar data will spread across the workforce for workers to use as they consider whether or not to take a job with a given employer and thereby encourage more firms to move in the high-road direction.

> *The lesson: Companies that are implementing high-road business strategies and high-performance work systems are essential for achieving a new social contract. They are critical if we are to once again see workers' incomes, employment conditions, and living standards advance in tandem with the productivity and profits they help generate.*

The problem is these practices and systems are not being diffused widely across American industries, and in fact their prevalence may have declined somewhat in the past decade. We don't have a clear understanding of why. Explanations (hypotheses, really) are varied: lack of information about how to implement these practices, the high start-up costs and delayed benefits they experience (sometimes called "worse before better" traps), failure to reform and modernize labor law to support these strategies, and the pressures from financial market agents to maximize short-term returns.

There may also be a market failure at work here. As employee tenure decreases and more parts of a firm's value chain are outsourced, the

---

[12] http://www.glassdoor.com/index.htm.

[13] http://www.indeed.com/.

incentive for an individual firm to invest broadly and deeply in the workforce also decreases. Indeed, the most recent fad in the human resource management literature is to emphasize "talent management" by focusing on key executives instead of investing in the firm's overall workforce. This may be rational behavior for an individual firm, but it is not optimal for building human capital across the value chain or across American industry.

Very likely all of these factors play a role. The net effect is a two-equilibria economy: some firms compete using high-road, knowledge-driven strategies, while others compete using low-road strategies that minimize labor costs. To date, more have chosen the latter than the former. Investment analysts are more schooled in evaluating low-road, cost-control strategies and have less of an understanding of high-road strategies and less data available to evaluate high-road firms. This puts high-road firms on the defensive and discourages others from following their lead. The key challenge is to tip the balance in favor of the former so that the low-road firms will be forced to upgrade their practices and employment standards in order to remain competitive. This will require overcoming the barriers and market failure noted above, and it will require coordinated actions among employers in the same industry and/or region. I will explore options for making this happen in Chapter 6.

Alternatives to the Public Corporation

The high-road/high-performance work system strategy relies on managerial leaders and, where present, union leaders who choose to adopt these practices because they believe they will work better to achieve the goals of the firm and the workforce. There is another approach, one that attacks the shareholder maximizing model directly by changing the corporate charter to be more inclusive of other stakeholder concerns. One such approach is called the benefit corporation.

Benefit Corporations

Benefit corporations are a new class of corporation that "(1) creates a material positive impact on society and the environment; (2) expands fiduciary duty to require consideration of nonfinancial interests when making decisions; and (3) reports on its overall social and environmental performance using recognized third party standards."[14]

At present, 31 states and the District of Columbia allow firms to incorporate with benefit corporation charters. The most important of these is the state of Delaware, since most companies around the country choose to incorporate in Delaware because it has the most fully developed set of corporate governance laws and regulations. As of 2013, an estimated 786 companies had been certified as benefit corporations.[15] One of the best-known examples is Patagonia, a California-based maker of hiking and other outdoor sportswear and climbing gear. When it incorporated as a benefit corporation, its founder, Yvon Chouinard, said:

> Patagonia is trying to build a company that could last 100 years. Benefit-corporation legislation creates the legal framework to enable mission-driven companies like Patagonia to stay mission driven through succession, capital raises, and even changes in ownership, by institutionalizing the values, culture, processes, and high standards put in place by founding entrepreneurs.[16]

To date little research has been done to assess how these organizations fare over time. Hopefully this will change, especially if their numbers continue to increase.

Employee Ownership

We the Owners is a 2013 documentary that tells the stories of people employed at several employee-owned enterprises across industries that

---

[14] "A New Class of Corporation," Benefit Corporation, 2015, http://benefitcorp.net/.

[15] Haskell Murray, "How Many Benefit Corporations Have Been Formed?" Socentlaw, July 23, 2013, http://socentlaw.com/2013/07/how-many-benefit-corporations-have-been-formed/.

[16] Mat McDermott, "Patagonia Becomes a California Benefit Corporation," treehugger, January 3, 2013, http://www.treehugger.com/corporate-responsibility/patagonia-becomes-california-benefit-corporation.html.

range from beer brewing to construction to manufacturing.[17] The stories of the workers in the film capture the promise of employee ownership advocates: When employees are and feel like owners, they will go the extra mile to contribute energy and ideas about enhancing the success of the enterprise. This will be a source of competitive advantage for the firm and a source of great satisfaction and financial return for the employee-owners.

Currently, there are over 10,000 employee-owned firms in the United States with an estimated total 12 million employees.[18] The evidence is quite clear about what conditions must be in place if employee ownership is to realize its promise. The key is that the culture of the organization must embody the theory of employee ownership and employees must actually have a voice in shaping how they do their work and how the operations of the firm might be improved. In addition, compensation systems must be designed so that bonuses or profit shares or longer-term equity growth are supplements to and not substitutes for a competitive wage. But if employee ownership is only a financial transaction or only provides seats on the board of directors for one or more employee-owner or representative, it is likely to do no better than its competitors at best and to eventually decline and fail at worst.

Employee ownership has some real advantages. It also has to be designed and managed carefully, as described above. Employees should never put all their eggs in one basket by investing all their retirement savings in the stock of their employer (obviously this advice holds true whether the firm is employee owned or not). Also, employees need to beware of firms that create ownership schemes largely or solely for tax advantages or the wage concessions they can gain by adopting this organizational form.

I can personally attest to examples of trucking firms that were in financial trouble in the 1980s that reluctantly accepted sharing a minority ownership stake with employees in return for wage concessions. I sat on

---

[17] See the trailer for *We the Owners: Employees Expanding the American Dream* at http://www.wetheowners.com/.

[18] Joseph R. Blasi, Richard B. Freeman, and Douglas L. Kruse, *The Citizen's Share: Putting Ownership Back into Democracy* (New Haven, CT: Yale University Press, 2014).

the board of directors of two such firms as a representative of the employee-owners. In neither firm was the top management committed to sharing control or empowering frontline workers, as is required for generating the benefits of increased productivity and a sense of ownership among employees. Both firms eventually had to be merged with others to avoid bankruptcy. There are other stories like this. The point is that employee ownership is a valuable and viable option for structuring firms in ways that give employees a stake in the enterprise. When a firm is managed as a truly employee-owned entity with high-road practices, it can and often does do well and realizes its promise. It would be wise to think about this as one good option for the future.

Cooperatives

Cooperatives are organizations owned by a large number of people or organizations that contribute key resources to make them work. Those of us who grew up on farms might remember their families being part of a milk cooperative or a feed store where they took grain and corn to be ground up and mixed with other good stuff to make healthy food their cattle loved to eat. Some well-known sawmills in Oregon have been organized as cooperatives for many years. At the other end of the spectrum is the Harvard (and MIT) Cooperative Society, a bookstore with branches on the Harvard and MIT campuses. And then there is my favorite cooperative-like organization: the Green Bay Packers! The Packers are owned by community residents who bought shares issued by the team so they could stay in business in the 1930s (and again to raise revenue to expand Lambeau Field in 2010). So cooperatives have a long and venerable history. They are governed by a board of directors that is accountable to the many owners.

A signal advantage of the cooperative form is that it cannot be sold or become subject to a hostile takeover by a financial investor seeking newfound, often short-term gains. Stability and continuity and presumably therefore a long-term view are built into this organizational form. (How else could Green Bay, Wisconsin, a city of about 100,000 people, have kept a professional, often a very good, and sometimes a championship football team for nearly a century?)

Perhaps the most famous and certainly one of the most successful cooperatives is found in the Basque region of Spain. The Mondragon Group is the world's largest worker-owned industrial cooperative. It was founded by a Jesuit priest in 1956 and has grown to employ 70,000 workers in Spain and another 15,000 in other countries in a variety of separate businesses in industries that range from auto parts to financial services, construction, and research. Large and successful cooperative firms are also active in other countries; these include Novo Nordisk (Denmark), Tata (India), IKEA (Sweden), John Lewis Partnership (UK), and Natura (Brazil). Thus, this organizational form is another alternative governance structure that enables multiple people to achieve multiple objectives, including goals related to profit and the welfare of the planet.

The key lesson to be taken away from this discussion is that the values, governance systems, strategies, and bottom-line objectives to which businesses are held accountable are not preordained by some iron law of economics or legal requirements. These are all choices that founders, executives, and those who share power in corporations make. Firms can be successful by following different strategies and values. The consequences, however, for employees and other stakeholders, including those who wish to be stewards of the environment, are predictable. Firms driven solely by the goal of maximizing short-term shareholder value are bad for employees, for communities, and for any other stakeholders who have interests other than those who are focused on maximizing shareholder values.

Global Firms: Can We Hold Them Accountable?

But, one might ask, can't firms shop the globe for the lowest-cost locations where they are least constrained by oppositional groups that might challenge shareholder supremacy? The honest answer to this is yes, at least for companies whose products and services can be manufactured or performed outside of a local market area. Your favorite restaurant has to have a local presence and serve you near home. But if it is part of a chain, some of its supplies are likely to be sourced globally. Firms that can transport their products to their customers from anywhere on the globe have many choices of where to source parts of their products and services. The challenge then becomes how to either work with or control global corporations. Here a little history of Nike might help identify the options for taking on this task—and the limits of those options.

Learning from Nike

Nike was one of the first multinational firms to figure out that it could manufacture most or all of its products sold in the United States in other countries. As far back as the 1960s, when Nike was founded, it pioneered a business model in which it designed and marketed its athletic gear and apparel in the United States but manufactured them in lower-cost countries. Its first stop in the search for low-cost production havens was Japan. That lasted about a decade before it realized that Korea was capable of producing high-quality shoes and apparel at a much lower cost. Within a decade, Nike had replaced Korea with a variety of lower-cost Asian countries such as Indonesia, China, and Vietnam.

This model worked extremely well for Nike. Its excellent marketing strategies (including signing up icons such as Michael Jordan for its commercials) and innovative products soared to the top of the sales charts in the industry and in returns to shareholders. By the early 1990s, however, a new problem had arisen. Some of its suppliers in the developing countries where Nike contracted out the manufacturing process began attracting increased media exposure and criticism for violating safety, health, and child labor standards. Nike's first response was "This is not our fault or our problem; these are contractors, not Nike employees." That response did not work. By the mid-1990s, Nike executives saw that as the media accounts increased, the company's stock price decreased. CEO Phil Knight famously said at one point that he was tired of the fact that "Nike's products have become synonymous with slave wages, forced overtime, and arbitrary abuse!"[19]

---

[19] Quoted in Richard Locke, *The Promise and Limits of Private Power* (New York: Cambridge University Press, 2013), p. 49. The material on Nike in this chapter draws from the research findings reported in this book.

Nike's decision to acknowledge its responsibility for working conditions throughout its supply chain sparked a major effort within the organization. Among other things, Nike:

1. Created a corporate social responsibility (CSR) unit and charged it with improving conditions in its supply chain and working externally with the media, academia, and customers to improve its image
2. Established a code of conduct—standards that it would expect all its suppliers to meet regarding issues that included child labor, safety and health, limits on hours worked, use of toxic substances, and compliance with environmental regulations
3. Sent auditors, either staff from Nike's CSR unit or consultants Nike hired, to audit selected suppliers to measure compliance with its code of conduct
4. Provided management advice to contractors on how to change their production and workplace processes so they could improve efficiency, quality, and employment practices
5. Began working with various NGOs that were active in publicizing labor standards violations in supplier firms and with NGOs that provided independent auditing services on the issue of labor standards
6. Shared its auditing data with selective and highly respected academics whom the company trusted but who also retained their independence and commitment to publishing the results of their analysis
7. Created a website (http://nikeinc.com/pages/responsibility) that made public the locations of its supplier factories, summarized the results of its audits, and reviewed progress and obstacles encountered in meeting its labor standards' targets
8. Met (at MIT and later at Stanford) with academics, other multinational firms, NGOs, and International Labour Organization officials in multi-stakeholder forums aimed at promoting "Just Supply Chain" practices

Nike was not alone in taking these actions. Other apparel firms, consumer electronics firms, and food and beverage companies came to the same conclusion: They had to respond to increased pressures from

NGOs and consumers by taking greater responsibility for the labor and environmental practices of their global suppliers. This opened a new avenue of research and debate among academics, labor representatives, and NGO activists working on these issues.

Were these so-called soft laws, or private regulatory efforts, successful in improving labor conditions in supplier firms or were they mere public relations facades? A team of MIT researchers led by Richard Locke has done the most extensive and widely acclaimed study of this question. He was the first trusted yet independent academic that Nike shared data with and worked with to learn from its audit experiences. Rick not only organized an army of graduate students to go with him into the field to see first-hand how the codes and all other aspects of Nike's efforts were working, he and his students also mined Nike's data to determine what factors accounted for the wide variations in auditing results they observed both in the numbers and in their plant visits. He was then able to get other companies in the apparel industry and later in the electronics industry to share their data with him. Over the course of a decade of research he concluded:

1. The initial pressure from NGOs was essential to initiating the chain of responses on the part of companies, international agencies, consumers, and members of the research community to this problem.
2. The codes of conduct and the audits had a positive effect on improving conditions but reached a plateau of somewhere between 50 and 60 percent on a scale where 100 percent would measure complete compliance with all the standards included in the codes. The standard violated most frequently: limits on hours of work and overtime. The standard most ignored or misreported: freedom of association. His conclusion from these data was that something was needed beyond compliance.
3. The suppliers that received management consulting help on a consistent basis scored better on the audit measures, as did suppliers located in countries that had stronger reputations for a rule of law—that is, those that had less corrupt governments, more human rights laws, and sound commercial laws.

Why, might you ask, are hours of work and overtime standards so hard to enforce? It is simple. The corporate staffers responsible for predicting which new items or styles of dress will take off and be hot items in a given selling season are not very good at their trade. They often can't anticipate fluctuations in demand accurately. So when they see signs that they have underestimated demand for something that takes off, they call their production colleagues and insist on getting more of the hot items as soon as possible. The pressures to deliver quickly then reverberate down through the supply chain to the contractors who are told, "Deliver what's needed now or you will lose this business and any future orders." The contractor then turns to his employees and says, "Deliver at all costs asap." The result: the contractor and his workers feel tremendous pressures to ignore the limits on hours and overtime that are written into the codes of conduct.

The lesson: Marketing and purchasing executives trump the CSR staff when it comes to questions of how to realize the profits to be made by meeting fluctuating and only partially predictable changes in consumer demand and consumer tastes. (Yes, that's us.)

A decade of research on these issues has led Richard Locke and most others who study these issues to conclude that (1) private regulatory efforts such as those pioneered by Nike and its peers are necessary but not sufficient to constitute a systemic strategy for monitoring and upgrading employment conditions in global supply chains; (2) assistance and technical support for management, strong labor, and employment laws that are enforced effectively and ongoing workplace representation institutions, whether they come from NGOs or labor organizations, are complementary and necessary elements of the system. We need to promote the use of all these elements if we are to continue to make progress in improving labor conditions in global supply chains.

But wait: Haven't we left an element out of the system? It is us— consumers. The evidence on whether we consumers are willing to help enforce global labor standards is mixed. Individually, those of us with sufficient discretionary income are willing to pay a bit more for some items if we are told they come from some certified source (think about coffee, chocolate, or other foods sold in upscale food stores such as Trader Joe's or Whole Foods). But overall, marketers do not perceive that the purchasing decisions of individual consumers send a signal that companies need to pay much attention to these issues.

However, don't tell that to those who are trying to sell athletic gear and labeled T-shirts and sweatshirts to big university clients where well-organized groups of United Students Against Sweatshops are active. Universities as diverse as Wisconsin, Cornell, and Brown have mounted successful boycotts against certain brands and insisted that those who produce their university-labeled apparel demonstrate that they are complying with acceptable labor standards.

> *The lesson here is obvious: While we as individual consumers need to do our part, the real power to change things comes when we, like these college student groups, band together in strategic ways that can make a difference. The United Students Against Sweatshops organizations that are active in big-market university athletic programs have shown the way.*

In recent years my colleagues and I have drawn on these two decades of experience and research in classes by focusing on the disastrous examples of suicides and poor working conditions that have occurred in Apple's supply chain, particularly in its largest supplier, Foxconn. The question we ask is "What should Apple learn from the earlier experiences of Nike in dealing with these problems?" Box 4.4 summarizes how one class answered this question in a letter they wrote and sent to Apple executives.

Box 4.4

Letter of MIT MBA students to Apple

To: Apple Inc
From: MIT Sloan 15.S06 Students
Date: March 6, 2012

Subject: Apple's Supplier Responsibility Crisis

Dear Apple Management,

As students at MIT Sloan studying Sustainability . . . we are concerned about the ongoing safety and fair labor standards violations documented in your Supplier Responsibility Report and in the media. We have carefully studied the steps taken by companies such as Nike to address these issues in their global supply chains and, based on this analysis, we would like to offer you the following recommendations as to what Apple can do to create more sustainable outcomes for all of its stakeholders.

Beyond Auditing

It is clear that Apple has recognized its strategic position as a powerful and influential customer and, commendably, has pushed its suppliers to open up their factories to external audits such as those conducted by the EICC [Electronic Industry Coordinating Committee]. That said, while such audits have been effective in exposing deficiencies in supply chain labor practices, systemic violations continue to persist.

We believe that Apple's suppliers may continue to miss the mark not because they don't want to improve, but because they lack the soft skills and know-how to manage extreme production pressures in a way that is consistent with Apple's supplier responsibility code. Apple can address this skills gap by building internal capacity for advanced Human Resource Management skills among its suppliers. As part of this initiative, Apple could:

- Ensure independent worker representatives have a voice in setting wages.
- Establish and enforce supplier sustainability metrics that are linked to performance, contract terms, and negotiations.
- Set up a joint venture with suppliers where certain production lines are used for the exclusive manufacture of Apple products and made by a joint team (i.e., akin to Apple's "store within a store" retail concept).

- Engage Apple's peers (other supplier customers) to jointly develop standards and monitoring for the global supply chain.
- Monitor and determine whether changes implemented to wages and labor conditions are commensurate with economic and social conditions and productivity levels of the various locations.

Structure Drives Behavior

While building supplier capacity to manage extreme production pressures is important, we also think it would be instructive for Apple to study the upstream business practices that drive production pressure and potentially create unintended and hidden costs to the workers who assemble Apple's products.

One such study could look at the industry tension between retailers' desire to hold minimal inventory and yet have immediate availability of stock to customers. Another could be to study Apple's own organizational architecture, and how its innovative style of independent teams can co-exist with the type of cross-organizational coordinated response that is usually required to address violations among suppliers. A couple of steps that Apple could take to align its organizational structure more closely with its supply responsibility goals include:

- Appoint a Global Lead of Sustainability who is responsible for monitoring the supplier situation, specifically overseas.
- Ensure that executives from purchasing and product development are equally accountable for upgrading supplier standards.
- Create HR/CSR hybrid roles where the individuals build labor partnerships with suppliers. This involves adopting "innovation teams," aimed at identifying the basic needs of workers (both inside and outside of the workplace), assisting suppliers in tracking productivity, cost savings generated from sustainability metrics, and so on.
- Develop new ways to incentivize employees to integrate supply chain innovations in their daily work.
  - o Build sustainability metrics into the internal organization's

balance score card/compensation model and employee performance evaluations.

   o   Create and formalize incentive programs (beyond direct compensation).

- Experiment with the way that products are built by integrating sustainability metrics into the product development cycle.

In closing, we feel that while this supplier crisis is severe, it also presents Apple with an opportunity to create a new global standard for supply chain sustainability, which in turn could be a source of competitive advantage for Apple and lead its peers to follow its leadership. We recognize the difficulties of quickly addressing ongoing supplier issues, controlling the supply chain pressures of delivering at the lowest costs, and monitoring business partners that operate within strict legal and political environments. However, with Apple's history of innovation, market power, and the leadership of Tim Cook, we hope that you will take this opportunity to create a new paradigm for supplier sustainability.

The lesson: Global corporations need to be held accountable by consumers, governments, labor organizations, international organizations, and NGOs to meet acceptable labor, safety, and environmental standards across their full supply and distribution chains. This requires a systemic approach that involves enforcing corporate- or industry-wide codes of conduct, effectively monitoring and enforcing systems, supporting efforts to build viable rules of law and effective enforcement regimes in host countries, and creating workplace institutions that promote effective management and give workers an ongoing role in the task of monitoring and upgrading employment practices.

CHAPTER 5

A New Age of Innovation?

Innovation obviously didn't stop when the door closed on the 1980s. And while we all often fool ourselves into calling the present moment an era of profound change and innovation, I'm going to take a risk and make just that claim. I'll leave it to some future historian to decide if I'm overstating the case. But in all my years of studying work, organizations, and labor management relations, I have not seen another era like the 1980s come along again until now. Let's see if you agree after I review some of the exciting changes in the start-up and entrepreneurship community, in large firms, in existing unions, in new emerging forms of worker advocacy some are calling "alt-labor," and in education. I'll even go farther out on a limb and suggest that we might be on the verge of another window of opportunity to bring about significant innovation in national policies governing work and employment. But that, you might decide, is wishful thinking.

Let's take a look at what is going on today.

The Sharing Economy

The term "sharing economy" is now used to cover a wide array of business models that use advanced forms of information technology to link consumers and service providers. Often these involve collaborative relationships such as Airbnb, a platform that allows people to rent out their homes and find other homes to rent while traveling. Nearly all of them disrupt existing business models in some significant way.

The most visible example of a disruptive new model is in personal transportation services, as illustrated by Uber, Lyft, and other companies that allow passengers to hire a taxi by using their smart phones. Uber, the largest and most controversial of these, is now located in 57 countries and is estimated to have a market value of over $40 billion.

I treated Uber as a case example of sharing-economy start-ups in the course and, not unexpectedly, the case generated a spirited discussion. Uber has a large and very loyal and enthusiastic customer base in the United States and, as I found out, in places as far away as China. Young people especially like the flexibility and speed of response time and the ability to use their smart phones to assess their options for getting a ride quickly and tracking drivers as they approach. A personal example in China brought home why this technology platform is capturing young people's attention and gaining market share so quickly. After a long day of teaching at Sun Yat Sen University in Guangzhou, China, my elderly (84 years old and still teaching!!) colleague and I were eager to get back to the hotel for a break before dinner and an evening class. Three of the students were assigned to get us to our hotel and were very attentive to my colleague, who has difficult walking. They said, "Don't worry, Uber is on the way." As we walked to the front door, all three were on their phones, checking on the progress of the driver. "Three minutes," they said, "so sit down here." Then, excited chatter among the three started with each looking at their phones like it was telling them something important. "No, four minutes," they reported. "Traffic is bad and the driver is headed for the wrong end of the building!" More chatter and clicking, and lo and behold, four minutes later the driver appeared in a five-passenger SUV, and our three competent students accompanied us to the hotel with a feeling of great satisfaction that they were taking good care of their elderly teachers!

Uber also has its critics, especially for the deal it offers drivers. Uber treats drivers as independent contractors, not employees. Drivers must meet Uber's hiring standards (which it raised after a number of scandals and tragic incidents). They must provide their own cars, which must meet Uber's standards (they cannot be more than seven years old), pay their own insurance, buy the gas, and set their hours of work. Uber sets the price of each trip, collects the fare via electronic payment, and pays the drivers about 75 percent of the revenue of each trip. While many drivers value the flexibility to choose their own hours (often as supplementary gigs to other jobs), some are protesting that Uber has cut the rates and income they receive. Other complaints are that the company unfairly shifts all the risks of the business to drivers, controls their work tightly via the customer ratings aggregated electronically in their files, and doesn't provide benefits such as car insurance, much less health insurance.

Driver critiques of Uber have not gone unnoticed. New worker-centered apps such as Sherpashare[1] have been created that allow drivers to input their revenue data, hours worked, expenses for gas, depreciation, insurance, and so on and calculate their real earnings per hours worked. Moreover, some drivers have tried to form unions, even though according to the outmoded U.S. labor law, as contractors, not employees, they are not covered by the law and therefore Uber has no legal obligation to bargain with them. Some drivers have challenged this exclusion, claiming that Uber controls so much of the way they work and the pay they receive that they should be classified as employees, not as contractors. Cases on this are weaving their way through various state regulatory agencies and courts and may end up being decided by the U.S. Supreme Court someday down the line.

Uber drivers are not the only people upset with the way the company does business. Certainly the cab drivers who work for traditional taxi companies are upset because Uber has started up in many cities under the radar of the regulations governing existing taxis. Bad experiences (including accusations of rape) have led some cities and indeed some countries to ban Uber from entry into their markets. Uber and other companies like it are now engaged in negotiations with a large number of cities and state regulatory commissions to try to work out these issues.

My students had a lively discussion about Uber. The comments below capture the different views expressed. As these comments indicate, there is great appreciation and acceptance of the value of this new service yet concern that it needs to deal with the low-road features of its business model.

> Flexibility is the main reason that I believe many people work for Uber. They are allowed to work multiple jobs and can also work whatever hours they so choose. I saw an Uber driver state in a video that he didn't work the night shifts because he couldn't

---

[1] https://www.sherpashare.com/about/.

deal with the drunk people who often damaged his car. He expressed pleasure with being able to choose his hours.

For many, not having a boss overseeing their every move is an advantage. They are free to go and work when they please without having someone telling them what to do and when to do it. This is especially good for those who may have other jobs or other responsibilities to attend to.

In order to better the working conditions for Uber drivers, I feel that possibly creating some sort of union could help them collect together for the same cause. When people come together in greater numbers, they can accomplish more. It's sad to read all the problems that Uber drivers have been facing. . . . I think that drivers need to demand more from Uber even though they are not employed with them but they still should be treated with more respect. They still work under Uber's brand name, so Uber should treat the drivers better in order to keep a good name.

Uber would be nothing without their drivers. I agree if they come together in a large number they can fight for better policies. A union could help employees such as the Uber drivers go on a peaceful strike to make the company realize how important it is to provide their somewhat employees with better working conditions.

Consider another example: Amazon's Mechanical Turk, an online job-posting platform for simple tasks related to information technology, and another app, Turk Opticon, that emerged as a source of leverage for those who accept and do the jobs offered on Amazon's electronic work platform. On Mechanical Turk, a prospective employer posts a task description and indicates the amount of pay (usually on a piecework basis) and individual workers can scan the available job offerings and pick one they feel competent and willing to do. Once the work is completed, the employer is obviously supposed to pay the employee. However, not all employers pay up, not all pay the amount promised, and not all pay quickly. This led an enterprising programmer to create a website called Turk Opticon that encourages employees to rate the reliability of those who offer jobs. People looking for jobs can review the ratings of potential employers before deciding whether or not to accept a job. A creative experimental study of the dynamics of this market has shown that the employer ratings have real effects. Good Mechanical Turk employers get their job offers accepted 100 percent faster than bad employers, and employees earn 40 percent more from good than bad employers.[2] This is another great example of using information as a source of bargaining power!

Uber and Amazon did not invent the sharing economy. In fact an early prototype might be e-Bay. It provided a marketplace where people can buy and sell a wide variety of goods online. Another prototype might be various automotive buying guides that provide all the information car buyers need before they visit dealers so they can bargain a fair price for a new or used vehicle.

A common feature of these business models is that they use easy access to information to change the relative power of the stakeholders involved. In the case of the automotive buying guides, car dealers lose some informational leverage over consumers. Uber uses information both to take business away from existing taxi services and to control drivers and customers. Sherpashare seeks to provide drivers with the information they need to assess the fairness of the bargain Uber is providing and therefore serves as a potential source of power, assuming drivers can collectively engage with Uber executives in some fashion. The key point is that these models can be designed in various ways. The question is why these entrepreneurs do not consciously build a consideration for other stakeholders—employees, for example—into their vision and business strategies. Uber did not, and neither did Amazon's Mechanical Turk platform. Both are now coping with apps that increase the bargaining power of their employees or contractors. We might ask why they don't adopt a high-road strategy right from the start and build consideration for these other stakeholders into the initial business model. We will see that efforts to encourage just that are under way in some segments of the start-up community.

---

[2] Alan Benson, Aaron Sojourner, and Akhmed Umyarov, "The Value of Employer Reputation in the Absence of Contract Enforcement: A Randomized Experiment," Working Paper, Carlson School of Management, University of Minnesota, 2015.

Start-Ups with a Social Purpose

So you are a young aspiring entrepreneur and want to turn your great idea into a successful business. You also want to build a sustainable company—perhaps in both an ecological and a social sense. But you know that at least in the early years of your new venture, money will be very scarce and it will be tough to attract the talented employees you will need and pay them a good salary. What do you do?

The evidence indicates that many who start firms either don't or can't provide really good jobs. Adam Seth Litwin and Phillip Phan have done the best research on this and found that most start-ups don't provide health insurance or pensions. Only 31 percent of the start-ups they researched offered health insurance and only 15 percent offered pensions, considerably lower statistics than we find at older and larger firms. Not a happy picture. But this picture is not preordained. The Litwin and Phan study found that larger start-ups, those that were better endowed (i.e., had a patent or trademark to build on), and those that were more profitable were more likely than others to offer employees both health insurance and pensions. So these features of start-ups make a difference.

The good news is that there seems to be a growing number of young entrepreneurs who share a passion for building environmentally and socially sustainable organizations that serve useful social purposes. And a number of organizations are working to help them do so. The mission of the Hitachi Foundation is to improve low-wage jobs. One of its programs supports young entrepreneurs who combine a passion for addressing some important social or environmental cause with the desire to build a profitable and sustainable new firm. The foundation works in partnership with organizations such as the Investors' Circle and the Social Venture Network to create spaces for young entrepreneurs to meet with investors looking for promising young firms with strong social missions. They are in effect creating incubators and mentoring processes modeled after successful high-tech incubators. You can find a set of videos describing some of these start-up businesses and the entrepreneurs who founded them at http://hitachifoundation.org/our-work/entrepreneurship-at-work-program. It is worth taking a look to see how creative, value-driven young entrepreneurs can make and are making a difference in a wide array of industries, from food and agriculture to education, health care, and alternative energy.

Innovations in Existing Businesses

Existing firms are not sitting idle waiting for smart entrepreneurs to disrupt their business models or worker advocates to become powerful enough to challenge them directly in collective bargaining. Indeed, in 2015 the pressures of the fast-food and retail industry campaigns induced companies such as McDonald's, Walmart, and others to announce their intention to raise wages above the minimums required in different locations. One company, Ikea, has gone farther and has committed to using a "Living Wage Calculator" created by MIT professor Amy Glassmeier to set wages for its store employees across the country.[3]

Starbucks announced in 2015 that it would offer its employees who lack a college degree tuition reimbursement. It also negotiated a lower tuition rate for online courses at Arizona State University. This is an example of a high-road move. It encourages employees to get a college degree that will enable them to advance (at Starbucks or elsewhere) to a higher-paying occupation and reduces turnover costs by holding on to these employees while they pursue their degrees. Microsoft made a comparable high-road move by indicating that it will require firms in its supply chain to provide sick leave for their employees. Presumably this will both increase the quality of work for employees affected and reduce delivery delays or increased costs associated with absenteeism among its suppliers. Dan Price, the CEO of Gravity Payments, a company that processes credit cards and gift cards, made a big media splash by announcing he would cut his salary and set a minimum salary of $70,000 for all employees.[4] His action generated lots of positive commentary in the media but highly critical comments from some business analysts. The critiques centered around the consequences of paying some of these

---

[3] Dave Jamieson, "Ikea's Minimum Wage Hike Was So Successful, It's Raising Wages Again," *The Huffington Post*, June 24, 2015, http://www.huffingtonpost .com/2015/06/24/ikea-minimum-wage_n_7648804.html.

[4] "Seattle CEO to Pay Employees $70,000 Minimum Wage," *USA Today*, April 15, 2015, http://www.usatoday.com/story/news/nation-now/2015/04/15/seattle-company-70000-minimum-wage/25810099/.

employees' salaries well above their "market wage" and the difficulty the firm might have in attracting capital from skeptical investors.[5]

A number of other large firms are encouraging their employees to pursue lifelong learning. A 2015 blog post cited nine large, well-known firms that offer attractive education benefits. Deloitte, for example, offers employees who have been with the company for two years free tuition toward an MBA and full support for classes that strengthen computing skills. UPS offers free tuition at local community colleges and technical schools to employees at its major hub in Louisville, Kentucky. Others on the list such as General Mills, Exxon Mobil, Proctor and Gamble, EMC Corporation, and Genentech provide similarly generous tuition reimbursement benefits. Clearly these and other large firms like them recognize the value of investing in their employees. Judging from the number of employees who have taken advantage of these benefits, the concept that lifelong learning is crucial in today's economy has taken hold.[6]

These examples suggest a good deal of innovation is under way in both start-up and mature companies. Among start-ups, the focus appears to start with mission-driven organizations that also want to improve job opportunities for low-income workers. Among mature companies, the current focus appears to be education benefits, and among some of the lower-wage firms, the focus seems to be on increasing starting wages somewhat in response to pressure from labor groups.

The question is how to build on this momentum to make it the norm across industries and to extend the innovative spirit to address (1) all workers and contractors who contribute to the success of the business; and (2) the full range of workplace practices that need to come together to achieve and sustain the productivity and fair wage outcomes of truly high-road firms. Perhaps a rebuilding of worker bargaining power, either in new or traditional ways, is what is needed to keep the momentum going. I turn to where things stand on this front below.

---

[5] Tom Duening, "Gravity's $70,000 Minimum Wage," Forbes, April 28, 2015, http://www.forbes.com/sites/tomduening/2015/04/28/gravitys-70000-minimum-wage/.

[6] Chris Couch, "9 Companies That Offer Fabulous Education Benefits," Schools.com, April, 17, 2014, http://www.schools.com/articles/companies-offering-educational-benefits.html.

Innovations in Unions and Worker Advocacy

A 2015 Pew Research survey found that young workers are more supportive of unions than any other demographic group. Fifty-eight percent of those aged 18 to 29 years have a favorable view of unions compared to the overall average of 48 percent. While this is a significant differential, it is still far from a ringing endorsement of unions by young workers, much less the overall population. Students in the online class expressed mixed views of unions. Some recalled bad experiences with unions that did little for them, some recognized the contributions unions have made in the past and their needed role in advocating for improved conditions for low-wage workers today, and some saw the need for new ways for workers' voices to be heard. Here is a sampling of what class participants had to say:

> I am surprised that you choose to include the story of the tear-jerker Milwaukee day care owner but fail to talk about the reasons a previously pro-union town like Milwaukee has elected officials that are obviously not "pro-union." Why not some discussion of the greed and corruption unions experienced in the 70s and 80s, the huge wage discrepancies between the union and nonunion jobs, the nepotism involved in trying to get a union job in Milwaukee, the concessions granted union workers which made union jobs the butt of many jokes around the dinner table? My brother-in-law had a union job at [a unionized company] during that time and he lived high on the hog, did very little work and generally enjoyed the good life while the rest of his family actually worked for a living. The pendulum had to swing back because unions took advantage of their collective bargaining power and were seen as being the demise of many good enterprising companies. This was after the generation of war veterans' kids began moving into the workplace[,] taking over the jobs their fathers held. They were entitled, fat[,] and happy. Yes they made up a great middle class in Milwaukee[,] but they met their demise because of greed. Not every job was a union job[,] and those that couldn't get in agreed with management that unions were a bad thing. Let's talk about the human nature of

greed, and what doing nothing for your salary does to those around you who have to put in sweat for their pay.

I believe low wage [workers] are still struggling and unable to get their voices heard without fear of losing out. I think one reason for this is the low number of jobs that still have a union standing by them and protecting them. Unions were an important role that allowed people to fight for what they want and I believe they should still be utilized today in many jobs because workers['] voices are important and workers are the backbone of every company.

Worker advocacy is something that is crucial in the workplace today. Today's workers have more rights than any other of the workers of past generations. This is largely due to workers using their voices[,] whether it be through social media or even through unions. It is very necessary and it is because of past workers advocating for rights, that current workers have as many rights as they do today.

I reckon that unions have to adapt to the changing work environment. I believe that in the past they focused too much on negotiations to get the best conditions to workers, but now I think that it's collaboration what is needed, how unions could spread the company's strategies and goals, so that everyone works to reach the same objectives, and in return how benefits would be spread across workers.

I think that there needs to be a balance between unions and companies. Obviously unions do a lot of positive work towards protecting the rights of workers and making sure they are not discriminated against by their employers. At the same time companies do need to protect themselves and not be bullied by unions looking for more and more benefits that might hurt the shareholders of the company. I believe there needs to be a mutual give and take between unions and companies that work towards benefiting the major needs of all parties involved.

Almost all union leaders now recognize that the labor movement is in severe crisis. Union membership in in the private-sector workforce has fallen to 7 percent, a level not seen since the years before the New Deal legislation of the 1930s. Like other crises, this one is spurring considerable efforts within the labor movement and by new worker advocacy groups outside of or only loosely allied with existing unions.

One of the early innovators is Freelancers Union,[7] formed in the 1990s by Sara Horowitz after she found out that her employer was classifying her as an independent contractor who was not entitled to the same rights and benefits as her colleagues. Today, Freelancers Union has over 250,000 members from a variety of occupations, including consultants, writers, nannies, and software developers. While it can't negotiate a collective bargaining agreement, Freelancers Union functions like a union in many ways. For example, it makes health care accessible for members and engages in political and policy activism.

Traditional unions are also looking for new ways to build their membership and establish relationships with employers that can benefit both workers and firms. The United Steelworkers Union, for example, promotes alternative corporate forms that involve employee ownership or worker cooperatives. In Portland and elsewhere, the Laborers' International Union has played a key role in training workers in skills needed for green jobs, such as brownfield remediation and weatherization of buildings. And the umbrella organization of labor unions—the AFL-CIO—has enrolled over two million nonunion workers through an affiliate called Working America[8] that does not engage in collective bargaining but provides information and mobilizes members in support of local and national policy issues and political initiatives.

A number of unions are also targeting some of the largest employers in low-wage sectors that heretofore have vigorously opposed employee efforts to organize. In 2012, a few hundred fast-food workers went on a day-long strike in New York City to protest low wages, irregular schedules, and poor working conditions. In 2015, this grew into organized one-day protests in 150 cities organized by the Service Employees International

---

[7] https://www.freelancersunion.org/.

[8] http://www.workingamerica.org/.

Union. Similarly, the United Food & Commercial Workers International Union, which organizes employees in grocery and retail stores and in the food-processing and meat-packing industries, created OUR Walmart, an organization of nonunionized Walmart employees who are working toward establishing higher wages, regular schedules, health care benefits, and respect on the job.

The AFL-CIO has created a young workers' group that meets at local levels across the country. In 2015 over 1,500 of these young activists came together in a national conference. The group also developed its own economic policy strategy called Common Sense Economics.[9]

Perhaps the biggest organizing efforts outside the formal labor movement are the worker centers now found in 225 different localities that support immigrant and other low-wage workers by providing training in job skills and English and legal assistance for workers who are injured on the job or are not being paid their full wages and, in some cases, helping establish baseline wage standards in their communities.[10]

Another visible and innovative new organization is the Restaurant Opportunities Centers United (ROC). ROC was created in New York City after the Windows on the World Restaurant in the World Trade Center was destroyed on September 11, 2001.[11] Its model of training, raising wages, improving working conditions, and promoting sustainable food standards has expanded to numerous cities nationwide. Through these activities, ROC aims to change industry-wide standards. Importantly, it also conducts research on the industry that becomes incorporated into consumer education campaigns that seek to make customers aware of working conditions in the restaurants they frequent and thereby serve as allies for food-service employees who are seeking better wages and conditions in this industry.

---

[9] "About 'Common Sense Economics,'" Common Sense Economics: What Everyone Should Know about Wealth and Prosperity, http://commonsenseeconomics.com /about-common-sense-economics/.

[10] Janice Fine, *Worker Centers: Organizing Communities at the Edge of the Dream* (Ithaca, NY: Cornell University/ILR Press, 2006).

[11] Saru Jayaraman, *Behind the Kitchen Door* (Ithaca, NY: Cornell University/ILR Press, 2013).

The National Domestic Workers Alliance is another example of a new and growing organization. The alliance brings together organizations that represent over 10,000 nannies, home health care workers, and housekeepers. Its local affiliates have made significant inroads into improving standards in domestic work. In states such as New York and California, for instance, their efforts have brought about the passage of a Domestic Workers' Bill of Rights, which provides for overtime pay, protection from discrimination, and paid leave days—what we usually think of as fairly typical or normal rights on the job.

Another area where labor-related organizing has flourished pertains to local efforts to transform employment policy in specific localities where public funds are used in economic development projects. These campaigns often tie provisions for wage standards, training, and hiring policies to development projects that are funded through taxes or public subsidies. Another strategy is to embed improvement in city-held contracts for services such as trash removal or recycling. The overarching goal of many of these campaigns, similar to what we see with worker centers, is to transform jobs in particular sectors or a local economy into high-road jobs.

Other worker advocates have negotiated with elected officials and in some cases with representatives of the business community to increase minimum wages, establish living wage targets, or provide community benefit agreements (agreements negotiated with private developers to hire local residents and contribute to other community improvements). Currently, over 140 cities and counties have living wage laws that bring local wages above the federal minimum of $7.25 per hour and tailor them to the local cost of living. One of the largest community benefit agreements was formed in 2004 between a broad coalition of community and labor organizations and the Los Angeles International Airport, which was undergoing an $11 billion modernization project. The agreement provided for $15 million in training funds, addressed environmental and health concerns related to airport traffic, and created increased opportunities for minority- and women-owned businesses. The LAX Community Benefit Agreement also contained provisions for training and hiring local residents, thereby ensuring that the economic gains from development are distributed throughout the community.

Perhaps the most ambitious new effort of this sort is The Workers Lab, an "accelerator" for new worker advocacy organizations that is modeled after similar accelerators for business start-ups. As conceived by David Rolf, the president of the SEIU local in Seattle, The Workers Lab provides seed funding to initiatives that show promise for rebuilding worker bargaining power in new ways, have the potential to grow to a scale large enough to generate improvements in working conditions for significant numbers of people, and have financial models that eventually can be sustainable without outside subsidies. In its first year, The Workers Lab funded four projects.[12] One of these is the Restaurant Opportunities Centers mentioned earlier. Another is CoWorker.org, an organization that helps individuals and groups organize campaigns to fight injustices at work through online petitions and other information-based strategies. A third is the Workers Defense Project, which educates immigrant workers and contractors about their rights and advocates for them about issues such as wages owed, improvements in safety and health conditions, and other basic labor standards. The fourth is WorkAmerica, an online recruiting network that links apprentices, vocational/technical schools, and employers in order to streamline the talent development and placement processes for those with critical skills in construction and health care.

This sampling of new forms of worker advocacy springing up today signals a growing realization that the decline of traditional unions is leaving a void that has taken a significant toll on workers, the economy, and society. Indeed, a growing body of econometric research is demonstrating that the decline of union membership is a significant cause of the increases in income inequality experienced in the past three decades in the United States and elsewhere.[13]

Despite all of this activity, three central questions loom large. Most of these efforts are resource intensive and there are questions about whether they can be replicated and expanded to reach large numbers of workers. Second, all of them have yet to figure out a business model that

---

[12] http://theworkerslab.com/.

[13] Bruce Western and Joseph Rosenfeld, "Unions, Norms, and the Rise in U.S. Wage Inequality," *American Sociological Review* 76, no. 4 (2011): 513–537.

provides a sustainable source of revenue. Third, none have yet demonstrated that the sources of power they draw on, as innovative as some of them have been, are adequate substitutes for the power generated through collective bargaining in years past. So the three questions David Rolf raised about power, scale, and sustainability remain as dominant challenges that these emerging forms of worker advocacy are facing. Perhaps the next generation of worker entrepreneurs will build from these examples and discover and create ways to meet these challenges.

Innovations in Education

American educators are coming under increasing criticism for not preparing the current workforce and the next-generation workforce to function at the levels U.S. companies need from their employees if they are to be competitive in a global economy. The good news is that these critiques are driving more innovation and change in education today than the country has seen in decades.

The clear and convincing evidence that investment in early childhood education pays significant dividends later in life in terms of both educational attainment and lower crime rates has led mayors and governors to look for new sources of revenue to pay for universal prekindergarten programs.

Innovation is also accelerating in elementary and secondary education, in large part fostered by competition from private charter schools, the carrots and sticks that come with the funds provided by the Obama administration's Race to the Top education program, and a determination on the part of some education leaders to demonstrate that innovation and improvements in student achievement can best be achieved through collaborative actions of teacher unions and school officials.

Massachusetts is a case in point. Spurred by the desire to demonstrate there is a better alternative to improving education than the attacks Governor Scott Walker has made on Wisconsin's teachers and other public sector employees, which have included eliminating long-standing collective bargaining rights for public employees and making deep cuts in budgets for public schools and the state's university system, a group of us in Massachusetts created the Massachusetts Education Partnership

(MEP), a consortium of leaders among the state's school superintendents, school boards, teacher unions, and state government that focuses on working together to drive improvements in student achievement.[14] In its first two years of activity, the group provided training and hands-on facilitators (neutral experts who help the parties use problem-solving techniques) for negotiating new labor agreements. It also provided intensive training for districts and local unions tackling specific problems such as extending the school day/year and implementing new teacher performance evaluation systems. It has worked in one way or another with leaders in about one-third of Massachusetts school districts. In the Boston public school system, this involved facilitating discussions among teacher union leaders, the school superintendent, and the mayor. The result was an agreement to add approximately one month's time to the school year. This was something the parties had failed to reach on their own in prior contract negotiations. So yes, Governor Walker, there is a high-road approach to innovation in education!

Universities are also on an innovative track that seeks ways to reduce the cost of college, reach large numbers of learners beyond their campus walls, and improve pedagogy for on-campus students via online learning technologies. Some are doing this in cross-university consortia, some are doing it on their own (such as the Arizona State University example mentioned above), and some are doing it in partnership with profit-making ventures (such as Coursera[15]). All are still in the developmental stage and are searching for sustainable models and the best ways to integrate on-campus and online teaching. My own view is that the biggest potential for online learning lies in working in partnership with industry groups to support the lifelong learning today's workforce needs in order to adapt to changing skill requirements and to help fill whatever shortages might occur.

Finally, I will discuss in some detail innovations that are under way to address the need for what is known as middle skills, or technical skills in areas such as construction, manufacturing, utilities, communications,

---

[14] Barry Bluestone, Thomas Kochan, and Nancy Peace, "Getting Along: A Better Approach to Public Sector Labor Relations—and Improving Schools," *Commonwealth: Politics, Ideas & Civic Life in Massachusetts*, April 14, 2015, http://commonwealthmagazine.org/author/thomaskochan/.

[15] https://www.coursera.org/.

and services. Industry is already concerned about a shortage of workers with such skills, and this shortage will intensify as the baby boom generations retire. I save this for last and discuss it in more detail because it illustrates a solution to a market failure that is currently constraining employers from investing in the training and workforce development that is needed to extend best practices or high-road strategies to a scale large enough to have a sizable national impact.

Beyond the Individual Firm: The Power of Business, Education, and Labor Consortia

There is a classic market failure at work that holds back the large-scale diffusion of organizational practices that have a proven track record in building good jobs and good profits. Those who buy into this market failure think like this: "If I invest in training my employees to be high performers but my competitors don't, they will hire (some say 'poach') my newly skilled employees away. The result is that I will bear the costs of my investments and they will reap the benefits."

The well-known key to overcoming market failures such as this is to get parties, in this case competing firms in a product market or regional labor market, to work together and share the costs of the investments and then compete to share in the benefits their investments produce. Indeed, a good deal of this type of cooperation is under way in regional and/or industry and occupational training programs. Just as we have learned much about what makes firm-specific work practices effective, research over the past decade or so has identified the key elements of successful efforts. Successful programs of this sort embody some or all of the following features:

1. Multiple employers in a region or an industry, sometimes in joint efforts with unions or professional associations, cooperate with one another and with educational institutions to design and fund initiatives to train and hire graduates.
2. Classroom education is integrated with opportunities to apply new concepts and skills in actual or simulated work settings—an approach that has been proven to be the way adults learn best.

3. Training focuses on offering workers career pathways in the occupation or with an employer, not just skills for an initial entry-level job.

Let's look at some of examples of promising programs embodying these attributes that seek to address the current and future need for middle-skill workers.

"Ecosystem" is a term often used to describe the mix of organizations, institutions, and people that need to coordinate their efforts to contribute to economic development, successful businesses, and good jobs within a community. One such ecosystem in Wisconsin Rapids, Wisconsin, is anchored by the Incourage Community Foundation and a consortium of employers and other community-based organizations called Workforce Central. A number of the region's major employers are members of this consortium, including its largest private employer, the Ocean Spray cranberry cooperative. Like many stories of economic development, this one grew out of an economic crisis: the loss of the paper industry that had served as an anchor industry in the community for decades.

Kirk Willard, the manager of Ocean Spray's Wisconsin Rapids plant, and Kelly Ryan, president of the Incourage Community Foundation, described at a recent MIT conference how they worked together to help recruit other employers in the region for a project to rebuild their vocational education school (with financial support from the National Fund for Workforce Solutions, a national consortium described in Box 5.1) and increase the technical and behavioral literacy, skills, and attitudes of the local workforce. By working with these funders, the local Ocean Spray plant has succeeded in growing jobs, improving its productivity and quality, and winning recognition as the company's best-performing plant for five years in a row.

This story, and many others like it, demonstrates that when employers work together, costs can be shared and intermediary institutions such as local vocational schools (in this case) and local community colleges can take on critical coordinating roles. (Sometimes these intermediaries are called "system integrators.") The benefits that accrue to participating firms and employees help revitalize local economies. A great example of an ecosystem at work!

Box 5.1

The National Fund for Workforce Solutions

The National Fund is a dynamic national partnership of communities, employers, workers, and philanthropists that serves 30 communities. It connects low-wage workers to the education, training, and credentials they need to secure access to family-supporting careers. Since 2007, National Fund workforce collaboratives have served 42,299 workers and brought together more than 4,060 employers to establish 151 work force partnerships across the country.

Source: National Fund for Workforce Solutions, http://www.nfwsolutions.org/.

Examples such as this can be found in many regions around the country. Box 5.2 summarizes several from a *Harvard Business Review* article my colleagues David Finegold and Paul Osterman and I wrote in 2012.

Box 5.2

Examples of regional training consortia

The Bay Area Workforce Funding Collaborative, founded in 2004, unites local governments, community colleges, and businesses in the San Francisco area. It has trained more than 700 unskilled and displaced workers for well-paid jobs with defined career ladders in the biotech and health care sectors.

Boston-based SkillWorks, founded in 2001, has placed more than half of the 500 displaced workers it has trained in new jobs. It has also upgraded the skills of more than 1,000 incumbent workers in health care, hospitality, property services, automotive services, and green industries.

The Wisconsin Regional Training Partnership (WRTP) includes unions, companies, and educational institutions. The partnership provides 40- to 160-hour training programs in technical and general skills for manufacturing, construction, and health care jobs. An experiment found that people who took part in the WRTP or other similar sector-based training had better outcomes than those in a control group of comparable people who were not in the WRTP: The WRTP participants were more likely to find steady jobs, work more hours, and earn a higher hourly wage. Indeed, they earned 29 percent more, on average, than the controls did in the year after the training.

Source: Thomas Kochan, David Finegold, and Paul Osterman, "Who Can Fix the 'Middle Skills' Gap?," *Harvard Business Review* 90 (December 2012).

We also reviewed examples of joint efforts organized on an industry or sectoral basis. One good example is the Center for Energy Workforce Development. In 2006, when the energy industry recognized that it faced a large number of retirements in the decade ahead (what some have called a "demographic cliff"), industry leaders formed a nonprofit consortium composed of electric, gas, and nuclear utilities; their trade associations; and the International Brotherhood of Electrical Workers. Leading firms in the industry such as the Georgia Power Company report that this program has created a pipeline of new workers to fill line technician and other skilled positions. It has also reduced its hiring and training costs by 31 percent and boosted employee retention from 75 percent to 93 percent. The resulting savings and increased productivity produced a sizable positive return on investment for the company.

Apprenticeships run by unions or by joint programs between unions and employers provide another example.[16] These programs combine classroom training with on-the-job experience. Completing registered training programs (the U.S. Department of Labor certifies apprenticeships that meet certain standards) has been shown to result in an average $250,000 increase in lifetime earnings for graduates and a 36 percent rate of return for the employers that help fund these programs. Unfortunately, the number of registered apprenticeship programs has declined by 36 percent since 1998 and the number of apprentice graduates has declined by 16 percent since 2003, in large part because of the decline in union membership. Reversing this decline should be a top priority for next-generation unions and professional associations.

---

[16] North America's Building Trades Unions, "Construction Apprenticeship: The 'Other Four-Year Degree,'" http://www.bctd.org/BCTD/media/Files/BCTD-Appren-Four-YR-Degree-2015.pdf.

Other unions and industry partners have developed training and career advancement programs tailored to their industry and their workforce. Health care is a prime example. The Service Employees International Union, which represents many entry-level health care workers (nurses' aides, food workers, cleaning staff, transport staff, etc.), has well-developed programs on both the East and West Coast. These programs offer opportunities for entry-level workers to gain certifications to move up the occupational ladder (e.g., moving from a position of nurse's aide to become a certified practical nurse) and to enhance health care workers' language, technical, and problem-solving skills. These skills are critical to serving patients and improving the quality and efficiency of health care within their occupations. One program that was jointly designed and managed by a union coalition and Kaiser Permanente offers 79 training programs of this sort and serves about 2,000 people per year. Participants who have advanced from licensed practical nurse to registered nurse though this program achieved a wage increase that was 18 percent higher than the across-the-board increase for all employees. Ninety-five percent of these nurses stayed more than six years with Kaiser, compared to 85 percent of other newly hired registered nurses.

Universities provide other models for joint industry-education partnerships that help overcome the disincentives for individual firms to invest in training or lifelong learning programs. Northeastern University, for example, enrolls over 90 percent of its students in cooperative programs involving 2,500 companies. MIT has had two industry-university joint educational programs, Leaders for Global Operations and the Systems Design and Management Program. The latter combines online learning with on-campus programming for engineers who continue working in their companies while they earn a joint masters' degree in systems engineering and management. Leaders for Global Operations provides a joint engineering and management degree for full-time students whose program includes a six-month internship in partner companies. Both programs are jointly funded by industry participants and have industry-university governing boards that work together to shape the curriculum and oversee the programs.

> *The key lesson from these examples: The market failures that hold back investments in training can be overcome when a company cooperates with key stakeholders such as other employers, education institutions, and employee representatives. Hopefully, the programs these joint efforts create will be models for many others to come in the future.*

These examples illustrate why I see this as such a promising innovative moment in history. If the market failure that is holding back investment in middle skills can be solved by cooperation among business, education, and labor, then perhaps we could foster other multistakeholder efforts to spread other promising high-road practices and business strategies.

But one player is missing—the big stakeholders in Washington! Is the political gridlock in Washington inevitable? Or might there be another opportunity like the one described in Chapter 2, when the New Deal arose after decades of evidence that a new public policy foundation was needed to support the transition from a farming economy to an industrial economy? Today another transition is long overdue: from an industrial economy to a knowledge- and innovation-driven economy. But if we are to achieve a policy breakthrough that is anything close to what is needed or is equivalent to the New Deal breakthrough of the 1930s, we had better first learn the lessons about why we have failed to make progress and let employment policy fall so far behind. The final section of this chapter will briefly look at two failed efforts at policy innovation with an eye to lessons that should guide efforts to do better the next time an opportunity presents itself.

Tales from Washington: Two Open Windows That Were Quickly Shuttered

Window 1: The Election of Bill Clinton

Recall that one of the events that triggered the breakdown in the postwar social contract was the government's failure to pass a mild form of labor law reform in 1978. Over the course of the 1980s it became more and more clear that America's labor law was failing and badly out of date. Moreover, it was not capable of supporting the innovations that were needed to generate high productivity and good jobs and diffuse high-road employer strategies across industry. Many of us who were studying these issues called for a new labor policy that was better attuned to the changing nature of work and the needs of workers and progressive employers. But alas, we failed. Here are two tales from these efforts and the lessons they offer for future efforts.

The months and years between December 1992 and January 1995 were among the most frustrating and interesting times of my professional career. They coincided with the opening and closing of the window for significant labor policy reform during the Clinton administration. By 1992, we had learned most of the lessons about the permanent changes in labor-management relations reviewed in earlier chapters. The traditional model of collective bargaining that had served the economy and the workforce so well and had created and sustained the postwar social contract was dead in the water, and debates over whether or not it would rebound were over. Or so I thought. That's why I wrote a memo to President Clinton's transition team and Robert Reich, the new secretary of labor, saying essentially, be bold and put in place a new labor policy that applies the lessons of the high-road/high-performance work system companies (and unions). (See Box 5.3) But whatever you do, don't set up some blue-ribbon study group to search for consensus over a new policy. There is no deal to be made between labor and management on this. Internal divisions will hold both groups back from being bold, and ideological differences between business and labor will only perpetuate the impasse. (Remember that in Chapter 2 I noted that there was no consensus to be found between business and labor right after the crisis period and the innovations that were invented during World War II.)

My advice, sadly, was ignored. Instead, President Clinton and Secretary of Labor Robert Reich chose (under pressure from AFL-CIO leaders) to create a Commission on the Future of Worker Management Relations, also known as the Dunlop Commission, after its chair, Professor John Dunlop of Harvard University. I was asked to serve as a member.

Box 5.3

Objectives for a mutual gains policy

(1) To support broader adoption of practices that contribute to a high productivity/high wage employment relationship, (2) to provide workers with an effective voice in decisions that affect their long-term economic welfare, and (3) to empower employees and employers to take responsibility for administering labor policies in ways that are suited to their particular circumstances.

To support these broad objectives labor policy should:

1. **Encourage Innovation.** Encourage innovations in employment practices and labor-management relations needed to achieve the full returns on investments in capital and human resources and the improvements in productivity, quality, and innovation needed to be competitive with high wages and good working conditions.

2. **Support Employee Voice.** Provide workers and their representatives with the opportunities to have a voice in the workplace, [in] human resource policies, and [in] strategic decisions that affect their long-term economic security and earning power and the competitiveness of their employers.

3. **Diffuse Best Practices.** Learn from and help diffuse the lessons from best-practice cases for transforming workplace practices that have demonstrated their value to firms and their employees.

4. **Encourage Participation.** Encourage experiments with a wider array of approaches to worker participation and representation than those available to employers and employees under current labor law. In addition to collective bargaining, these would include informal problem-solving teams, labor-management consultative committees, enterprise councils, and employee representation on ESOP (Employee Stock Ownership Plan) committees and corporate boards of directors and cross-firm labor-management consortia.

5. **Encourage Self-Regulation.** Encourage workers, unions, and employers to take responsibility for administering policies such as occupational safety and health and employee training and

development, thereby reducing regulatory requirements and adapting the policies to the parties' needs.

6. **Ensure Workers' Right to Choose.** Provide workers with effective rights to choose the form of representation best suited to their particular circumstances and remedy any demonstrated weaknesses in laws or administrative procedures that limit workers' rights to join a union or engage in collective bargaining or other types of employee participation and representation free of discrimination, coercion, or fear of reprisal.

Source: Thomas Kochan, memorandum to Secretary of Labor Robert Reich, February 8, 1993, in author's possession.

To make a long and sad story short, we spent two intensive years in national and regional hearings taking testimony from countless leaders of labor groups, women's groups, immigrant groups, civil liberties groups, business community leaders, and experts on labor law. Most of the first year was spent convincing our chair, Professor Dunlop, that the world had changed and a new approach to labor policy that endorsed employee participation was needed. Eventually, we issued a first report that outlined the parameters of a new model and the evidence that supported it. But by the time we issued our final recommendations in January 1995, the window of opportunity had closed. The Newt Gingrich revolution had turned Congress over to Republicans who would have no part of labor law reforms except for a meaningless idea the business community liked because it promoted management-dominated teams. Gridlock continued.

Window 2: The Election of Barack Obama

Like many Americans, I was enthralled by the historic election of the first African American president in 2008. Barack Obama entered office because the country sorely needed new ideas and he articulated the hope of so many people for change—young and old, black and white, men and women. I thought we had a second window of opportunity to fundamentally transform labor and employment policies so we could finally catch up with the changes in the workforce, in the economy, and in the nature of work.

Although a number of us on the Obama Transition Team argued for a transformative agenda, a much more conventional approach to labor policy won out. In fact, labor policy was a backwater issue that gave way to the higher priorities of stabilizing the financial system, passing an economic stimulus bill, passing a health care reform bill, and countless other issues the administration deemed to be more important. The one labor policy idea the White House entertained was one that was being pushed as the labor movement's top priority, the Employee Free Choice Act, which would have made it easier for employees to form and join unions. That bill was doomed from the outset by the labor movement's insistence that workers could get a union to represent them by signing a card authorizing a union to represent them instead of requiring a secret ballot election.

Like most researchers who studied these issues, I was sympathetic to the reasons why labor was pushing this particular reform. The existing labor law is so badly broken and so subject to manipulation by smart labor lawyers and consultants that it effectively denies employees access to what our labor law promises them: that they, as employees, should be able to decide whether or not they want to be represented by a union and engage in collective bargaining. That is the intent of the law, but it is not the reality on the ground. Today, any employer who chooses to fight the efforts of workers to form a union has an expected rate of success of 90 percent. One of our PhD students, John Paul Ferguson (now a professor at Stanford), showed that less than 10 percent of organizing efforts make it to the final destination of achieving a collective bargaining agreement if management resists.[17] Such is the reality of labor law today.

But the notion that a bill that included card check union recognition could win in a political contest in Congress, even with a majority Democratic Senate and House, was foolhardy. And the Obama administration took a largely hands-off approach by letting labor see what it could do to build support for the proposed legislation. In the end, labor could do nothing and the bill fizzled out.

---

[17] John Paul Ferguson, "The Eyes of the Needles: A Sequential Model of Union Organizing Drives, 1999–2004," *Industrial and Labor Relations Review* 62, no. 1 (October 2008): 3–21.

The saddest part of this story is that the Obama administration had no labor policy of its own! The secretary of labor was one of the last cabinet positions filled. The Department of Labor was given no leeway to initiate policy proposals or to do the type of in-depth analysis of policy options that were necessary if a serious agenda was to be put forward. Instead, all labor policy decisions were centralized in the White House staff, which is comprised of economic and political advisors. The message was clear: If labor or some other group could muster support for something, it would be dealt with seriously. Otherwise, the White House economics and political team had bigger fish to fry.

Once again, a window of opportunity to bring about significant labor policy reform was lost. The death knell of labor law reform was dealt when Massachusetts replaced the late Senator Ted Kennedy with Republican Scott Brown. That ended any hope that Republican filibusters of labor-backed proposals could be overcome. Gridlock lives on.

I summarize these failed efforts to bring home a clear lesson:

The next time a window of opportunity opens, there should be no holding back. It will not last long and the agenda for action needs to be ready, just as Frances Perkins was ready to act on her New Deal agenda as soon as President Roosevelt took office and she walked into her job as secretary of labor. No study group for her. Hopefully, no more wasting time with "study groups" in the future!

Since I believe there may be an opportunity coming in the near future, a good deal of the last chapter will be devoted to laying out a narrative, agenda, and strategy for updating national employment policies in ways that will secure a positive future for members of the next generation.

Summary

Where do these innovations that span from the 1980s to today leave us? I believe that the seeds of innovation have been laid. We have learned much from the best-case examples of successful models of workplace transformation and from unsuccessful efforts to spread and sustain these innovations. We know which mix of high-road practices, tailored to the specifics of different industries, can produce better joint results for both shareholders and employees than low-road strategies. Companies that use low-road strategies might be able to match the profits and short-term shareholder returns of high-road firms, but such strategies are destined to keep wages low, unions out of the picture, and opportunities for learning and satisfying jobs frustrated. We also know why efforts to reform public policies that govern work have failed. If we remember the lessons learned from what made the social contract work well from the 1940s through much of the 1970s and build on the successes and failures of the years since 1980, we can begin to fashion a strategy for the future.

CHAPTER 6

A Call to Action: Building the Next Generation Social Contract

Here we are with a labor market that has been healing very slowly on the quantity front and only grudgingly in miniscule ways on the quality front, a political system mired in gridlock, a global economy in which jobs and wages are in fierce competition, and digital technologies that some fear will be the end of jobs as we know them.

But we have been here before, and thanks to the leaders who took action during and after the Great Depression, new national policies, institutions, and practices were put in place that laid the foundation for a social contract that served American society well for three decades. We can do it again by working together to build the next-generation social contract.

The good news is we have lessons to learn from the old social contract and from a host of innovations currently in practice that suggest ways forward. The challenge is to figure out how to build on what's working and identify what else is needed. In doing so we have to take into account and address the realties that were discussed in prior chapters. These include (1) globalization of markets; (2) advancing technologies that will both destroy jobs and create new opportunities; (3) variations in employer organizations and in the goals and strategies they pursue; (4) the decline in bargaining power and voice of workers; (5) the gridlock in national politics; and (6) market and institutional failures that employers and other stakeholders need to overcome through coordination and collective actions.

The underlying message here is that the key groups that share an interest in and responsibility for shaping the future of work need to reengage and work together in new ways. That is how a social contract can be achieved, by each party taking responsibility for its part and working with the other parties to forge agreements and address problems where joint efforts are required.

I will illustrate what we have in mind by drawing on an exercise from the online class at MIT, a simulated negotiation of the next-generation social contract. Then I will draw on what we have learned about what the parties individually and collectively can do to build a high-road economy; that is, one in which successful businesses that provide good jobs and careers are the norm, not the exception. I will challenge leaders from all the key stakeholder groups—business, labor, government, and education—to work with the next-generation workforce and with each other to fashion a new social contract that will be as durable as the one that ushered in decades of shared prosperity in the middle of the twentieth century.

The Next-Generation Social Contract Negotiations and Results

I used an exercise in the online class I called "Negotiating the Next Generation Social Contract" to simulate the multiparty dialogue and coordinated effort that will be needed to put the economy back on a more inclusive track. I present the results of our students' exercise not because they provide the answers to what needs to be done but to illustrate the potential for such an exercise among the real players who can make a difference.

The exercise had two phases. In phase one, participants were assigned to one of four stakeholder roles as leaders of the next generation: workforce, business owners, government officials, or educators. Each representative was then asked to rank order priorities among a set of issues that might be featured in a new social contract. In phase two, these representatives engaged with each other to see if they could negotiate agreements that should be part of a next-generation social contract with one or more of their counterparts.

Priorities

Figure 6.1 shows the priority rankings of each stakeholder group. There is a remarkable degree of consensus across groups. (Higher bars signify higher-priority rankings). For example, all groups give high priority to enhancing workforce capabilities and skills. There are also some obvious and predictable differences. Next-generation workforce representatives/unions rank fair treatment and representation for workers at the top of their priority list; employer representatives rank organizational performance as their top priority. There are also some interesting two-way pairings that illustrate the potential for bargaining among these stakeholders. Education and business leaders, for example, share high ratings for the issue of improving workforce capabilities. And education, government, and workforce representatives presented equivalently high rankings for the issue of the need to improve workforce rewards—wages and benefits. So let the negotiations proceed!

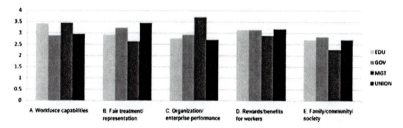

Figure 6.1 Stakeholder priorities for different issues

Negotiated Agreements

Figure 6.2 provides examples of the types of agreements generated by participants. Since the class was exposed to much of the material covered in the previous chapters, the range of agreements reached will look rather familiar. In the workforce capabilities category, agreements to support lifelong learning and pre-kindergarten education dominated. In the fairness and representation category, negotiators took up the need to find new ways for workers to have a voice through new corporate governance arrangements using data and reporting to hold corporations accountable for employment standards in the United States and abroad.

They also indicated support for collaborative partnerships between next-generation unions and companies. When it came to the tough issues regarding rewards and enterprise performance, these negotiators focused on the sweet spot of profit sharing and programs that support productivity improvement. In addition, they found ways to agree on fair but not uncompetitive norms for raising base wages—harkening back to the need to get productivity and wages once again moving together. In the area of family, community, and society, preference was given to respecting the next generation's priority for paid leave programs that would support balancing work and family responsibilities.

Issue Cluster	Settlements--Examples
Workforce Capabilities	Lifelong Learning
	Pre-K Education
Fairness	Worker Representation on Boards
	Accountability
	Labor Management Partnerships
Enterprise Performance	Productivity Improvement
	Flexibility to Adapt
Compensation and Rewards	Profit Sharing
	Fair Wages for Employees
Family, Community, and Society	Work-Family Integration (Balance)
	Maternity and Family Leave

Figure 6.2 Examples of agreements reached by issue cluster

Overall the results of this simulation illustrate the possibility that through engagement informed by knowledge of today's realities and shared information about priorities and viable options, leaders of these diverse stakeholder interests could forge constructive agreements. I now turn from the world of simulation to the real world and suggest what actual leaders of these groups might do individually and with others to forge a new social contract that can support good jobs and careers and put the economy on a path of sustained, shared prosperity.

Business Leaders

I start with the interests and expectations of future business leaders because throughout this book I have stressed that having more high-road businesses is the key to creating and sustaining good jobs and careers for the next-generation workforce.

Interests and Expectations

First and foremost, business leaders will need to manage organizations in ways that will achieve high productivity and long-term profitability. But as business leaders, citizens, and parents, they also want to provide good jobs and careers for future generations. Throughout this book I have stressed that it takes a mix of well-crafted high-road strategies and work practices to achieve both sets of objectives. This strategy in turn requires availability of a skilled, talented, and engaged labor force. But it is hard for any single business leader to meet all these goals and expectations acting in isolation. Business leaders need to work with each other and with leaders in government, education, and labor. Let's look at how they might go about achieving their interests and meeting the expectations that others in society have for business enterprises.

Options and Actions

> [Government leaders] do not realize that the corporate goal of profit maximization at all costs does not serve the interests of the nation. They do not realize that the fundamental goals of the country and of our companies have diverged. The sole focus on profit maximization, which leads to offshoring and holds down wages, does not serve the nation. . . . We must act to realign the goals of company and country.
>
> Source: Ralph Gomory, "A Time for Action: Jobs, Prosperity and National Goals," *Huffington Post,* January 25, 2010.

Ralph Gomory is a former chief scientist for IBM and the retired president of the Alfred P. Sloan Foundation. Gomory is one of the most thoughtful and credible critics of the narrowing of corporate goals that has taken place over the past several decades. He speaks from experience. He helped build a strong long-term research and development program at IBM and then created and oversaw an industry competitiveness program at the Sloan Foundation. His experience and wisdom as a thoughtful business leader give his words great credibility.

Gomory joins the growing chorus of voices suggesting that the financialization model of the American corporation has run its course and needs to be replaced with a broader view and that the new model must be complemented by strong and effective institutions in government and in civil society. But no one should have any illusions about how difficult this will be. One of the most powerful CEOs in the financial services industry made the obvious counterpoint at a Competitiveness Summit held at the Harvard Business School in 2011. After listening to Harvard professor Michael Porter speak of the need for firms to support efforts to enhance U.S. competitiveness and living standards, this executive commented: "I hear what you are saying, but every time I stand up and say we need to take actions to strengthen the U.S. economy, my shareholders cut my neck off, reminding me we are a global company." His point was not that he was personally opposed to taking a longer-run approach or to reinvesting in order to grow jobs and strengthen America's competitiveness. Instead, he spoke the truth about the countervailing pressures he is under from his shareholders and the financial agents and institutions that speak for them. So the question is: How can this transformation in corporate objectives and behavior be achieved?

Changing the values and behavior of the business community will not be easy. The key is to accept the statement of the financial services CEO that it is not in the self-interest of any single firm to invest in creating new jobs in the United States and that the quality of jobs they do create will depend on whether they choose a high-road or low-road strategy to compete. But as Gomory argues, we should not let corporate leaders off the hook. It is in the collective interest of business leaders to take actions to create more jobs in general and more high-quality jobs in particular. U.S. multinational firms still get about 60 percent of their revenue from domestic sales. This means that they depend on a strong, vibrant U.S. economy and on U.S. customers who have the incomes to buy their products and services.

Thus, we have a classic market failure problem. Focusing solely on maximizing the profits of firms creates costs that then have to be absorbed by society, while a process in which business owners worked together with other stakeholders to share these costs would generate mutual benefits. So the key lies in mobilizing business leaders to work with each other and with the government and civil society leaders who share an interest in and responsibility for the incomes, purchasing power, and standard of living of the country's next generation.

Where to start building this type of business community? Let's apply the principle that most of America's social and economic innovations have started at the local level. As we saw in Chapter 5, regional consortia of business leaders working with community colleges and vocational schools have demonstrated their ability to overcome the market failures that hold back individual firms from subsidizing their employees' education at local institutions. Model programs that mobilize groups of employers, such as those in California, Wisconsin, and other states, have demonstrated that it is possible to meet the needs of local employers and at the same time provide career opportunities with good rates of return for both employers and workers.

Apprenticeships and other joint union-management training programs also provide good opportunities for both employers and employees. In Chapter 5, I noted how employers and unions in the utility industry looked ahead and saw the demographic cliff coming a decade ago as its skilled labor force approached retirement age. The industry's joint training and apprenticeship program is now producing the next generation of technicians and repair workers. These workers can look forward to good-paying jobs and careers. When individual firms cooperate with each other to create such programs, they all benefit. Firms have access to the skilled and highly trained employees they need in order to remain competitive in their industry. The return on their investment in recruiting and training is much greater than it would be if each firm tried to create such a program on its own.

The same potential exists for businesses that need employees with the higher-level technical knowledge and skills that could be provided by colleges and universities via cooperative arrangements, online courses, and sponsored degree programs. As noted in Chapter 5, numerous companies have worked together with programs such as Northeastern University's Cooperative Education and Career Development program (http://www .northeastern.edu/coop/) and MIT's Leaders for Global Operations program (http://lgo.mit.edu/) to generate a steady stream of college graduates and postgraduates with state-of-the-art technical and managerial educations and direct experience with applying this knowledge to real problems in industry. The explosion of online courses provides an opportunity to take these examples to scale around the country. Doing so will go a long way toward reducing the costs of education and supporting the lifelong learning needs of the next-generation workforce and providing employees who have the skills industries are looking for.

Putting High-Performance Principles to Work

Attracting and training the talent companies need are only the first steps. In order to be employers that are attractive to the next-generation workforce and to be successful, sustainable businesses, companies will need business models and employment systems that have demonstrated a capacity to build truly high-performance organizations that depend on and sustain good jobs. The generic features of high-performance organizations are well known. We learned them from innovators as diverse as Saturn, Southwest, Costco, and Market Basket—workplace environments characterized by high levels of trust; employees and teams that are engaged in solving problems, making continuous improvements, and going the extra mile to serve customers; fair, competitive compensation levels supplemented with rewards that are tied to organizational and broader economic performance; and long-term business strategies that reinforce and support these employment systems.

Every industry in America, from high tech to health care to manufacturing to hospitality, provides examples of companies that have adapted these generic practices to fit their specific technologies and missions. The companies that learn to manage in this way will be successful in attracting and retaining the talent that is needed to sustain this business model. Those that fall short will put their reputations at risk and/or be engaged in constant battles to try to control and hold down the wages of a disgruntled and less talented workforce.

The standard corporate form is not the only governance model that is available to next-generation organizations. Entrepreneurs and leaders of existing companies need to consider the full range of governance models, including benefit corporations, cooperatives, and broad-based employee ownership.

All of these supportive organizational strategies and governance models would spread more widely and rapidly if powerful institutional investors and their agents were more diligent in asking about these company strategies, demanding data to measure their effects, and allocating funds to those with the most potential for achieving long-term profitability with good jobs. Some union pension funds are leading this charge. Some small initiatives such as the AFL-CIO's Building Investment Trust invest in projects that are built under fair labor standards and are managed in ways that generate competitive investment returns. Some giant pension funds such as the California Public Employees' Retirement Fund engage in sustainable investment strategies. A number of "impact investors" have demonstrated they can fashion sustainable strategies by putting together portfolios that favor companies that are both successful and have strong track records in terms of environmental responsibility and employment practices. The next generation of investment analysts needs to learn how to assess firms and hold them accountable for engaging in high-performance, long-run strategies that give equal weight to people and profits.

Business leaders (and, as I will argue below, government agencies) that invest globally need to also implement and enforce fair labor standards for all workers who contribute to the products and services they purchase. The lessons Nike and other companies learned in the last decade indicate that this is best achieved by working with NGOs, international unions, agencies such as the International Labour Organization, and host-country governments to monitor and enforce internationally accepted labor standards. The pressures to take these steps have come from student groups such as United Students Against Sweatshops and from the negative publicity about tragic experiences in global supply chains. The experience gained when these various institutions and organizations work together to monitor, improve, and report on progress in addressing these issues offers companies an opportunity to build this into their marketing strategies—but only if the efforts are real and effective. Judging from the views expressed in the letter the MIT Sloan MBA students wrote to Apple's CEO, there will be no shortage of young, committed professional managers ready to help steer companies in this direction. Let's put the next generation of managers in charge and watch them generate positive returns for all involved!

The Next-Generation Workforce

Interests and Expectations

The next-generation workforce needs to be well prepared to contribute to a high-road economy and employers. It also needs to be powerful enough to incentivize more firms to move in the high-road direction. The survey results reported in Figure 1.7, comments from students in the online course like those reported in prior chapters, and priority rankings in the negotiation exercise discussed above suggest that next-generation workers are ready and willing to do this. They want to address big problems and work in flexible ways to achieve a sensible work-life balance. At the same time, they share the interest of previous generations in earning a fair and decent living, having a voice in how they work, and feeling good about the relationships they build with co-workers, managers, and the customers they serve.

These data map well with what other surveys and studies of the so-called millennial generation have found.[1] Perhaps the best summary of their interests and aspirations is that they have an expanded set of expectations—they want the same things previous generations wanted from work and more.

Responsibilities and Options

Realizing these expectations has to start with the workforce itself. So let's examine what employees need to do to be productive contributors to the workplaces of the future.

---

[1] For one example, see "Mind the Gaps: Deloitte Millennial Survey 2015," http://www2.deloitte.com/content/dam/Deloitte/global/Documents/About-Deloitte /gx-wef-2015-infographic-millennial-survey.pdf. For a more extended discussion of what millennials want from work, see Lauren Stiller Rikleen, *You Raised Us—Now Work with Us: Millennials, Career Success, and Building Strong Workplace Teams* (Chicago: American Bar Association, 2014).

Next-generation workers know that the place to start is with a good education, but in their case education has to be a more continuous process, not a phase that one completes prior to entering the workforce. The mantra each generation has heard to "get as good an education as you can" is still a necessary starting point, but it is not enough. Today's students and members of the workforce not only need to work hard to get the best education possible, they also need to acquire the knowledge and skills that are in high demand and continue on a path of lifelong learning throughout their careers.

Not everyone will be able to afford or be ready to enroll in a four-year college after completing high school. Some will prefer to pursue technical jobs and careers via vocational schools, community colleges, and/or apprenticeship programs, and some will go to four-year universities. Regardless of which post–high school educational option is chosen, it must lay a solid foundation for a career of lifelong learning.

The career planning exercise used in the online course started with a tool young people could use to explore where the job and career opportunities of the future are the brightest and which ones will allow them to put their individual aptitudes and passions to work. I encouraged students to discuss their interests with people who were doing work that interested them and to look for educational programs that provided pathways into their careers of interest. The evidence on what to look for is clear: educational programs that are tightly linked to industry mentors; programs that provide on-the-job apprenticeships, internships, or other learning opportunities; and programs that have well-established pathways to jobs and careers after graduation. Young people need to do their homework and choose programs that have these attributes.

There are good tools available for doing so. Participants in the online class used the U.S. Department of Labor's online tool, the O*NET Interest Profiler,[2] to plot their personal career development plan. The Interest Profiler is particularly helpful because it provides a short (and free) questionnaire to assess one's career interests and occupational aptitudes and then uses those data to generate a range of occupations one might consider and the education required for different levels of jobs and salaries within each occupation.

---

[2] http://www.mynextmove.org/explore/ip.

Class participants put this tool to good use. Box 6.1 provides summaries of a few of the career development plans students produced.

Box 6.1

Career development plans sampler

PhD in chemical engineering: Values freedom and flexibility; wants to work in industry and then in academia and have a small consultancy as well. Plans to rely on networking, online courses, and additional classroom learning to get the certifications needed to move across these occupations over time.

Student in college: Target first job would be in communications, public relations, or fund-raising for a nonprofit. Wants to move up to be a fund-raising manager. Also wants to develop a nonprofit to help children develop their STEM skills. Needs to finish college and get registered with a professional regulatory body and perhaps join a union or professional association within his field.

Student in culinary school: Wants to be a personal chef. Needs to finish training, get registered, learn bartending and other server skills, practice knife cuts. Gets information about good jobs by reading customer reviews and going to restaurants.

Education professional who relocated to another city to help with caregiving for wife's 89-year-old mother: Continuing to read and self-educate to learn Spanish. Wants to work with kids in need. Evaluates prospective employers not just for the quality of the job they offer but also for whether they provide the resources needed "to connect diverse and disadvantaged families with the school district and to empower them to be partners with teachers in the education and success of their children. This [includes] funds for supplies and mileage, replacement computers, training, extra hours to provide family learning and access to staff, and the occasional lunch on me."

Budding politician: Needs to learn about international development; needs to work with nonprofits and do good work before entering politics; needs to avoid conflicts of interest regarding parents' business, then get into politics. Also needs to consider "my relationship with girlfriends, to try to maintain regular contact despite busy work schedule"!

Entrepreneur: Now in a PhD program in computer science. Will do various free services such as sponsor "hackathons" to identify start-up opportunities.

Filmmaker: Finish education, join relevant union, network.

Business developer: Needs to continue education through online courses and get an executive MBA.

Entry-level employee: Wants to eventually run a business—needs to take more courses in business administration, finance, and human resources and attend conferences for networking and learning and be prepared to "move where the customers are."

Substitute teacher: Needs to get California credentials—taking online courses.

PayScale, a web-based survey organization, provides additional useful information by publishing a list of the top 10 college majors that are most likely to lead to underemployment after a student graduates with a bachelor's degree. Table 6.1 provides the list, including the percentage of degree holders in different fields of study who are underemployed. While we might not take these numbers or even the specific rankings too seriously, the point is clear: Choice of college major does matter. This is not a reason to avoid a major of deep interest. Young people should continue

Table 6.1 Percentage of underemployed college graduates by field

1.	Criminal justice	62.4
2.	Business administration	60.0
3.	Health care administration	57.6
4.	General studies	54.5
5.	Sociology	52.5
6.	English language and literature	52.1
7.	Graphic arts	51.5
8.	Liberal arts	50.3
9.	Education	50.0
10.	Psychology	49.5

Source: "The 10 Most Underemployed Majors," Forbes.com (using data reported by PayScale), http://www.forbes.com/pictures/fhhk45gjll/the-10-most-underemploye/.

to follow their passions as undergraduates and get as broad an education as possible. The key is to come out of undergraduate school with an ability to continue learning—either by enrolling in graduate school on a full- or part-time basis or by taking advantage, perhaps with the help of employers, of the growing number of online courses being offered by various universities.

Universities and community colleges are eager to develop markets for their online courses. This offers a second chance to those who may not have chosen undergraduate degrees that are good matches with the technical or behavioral knowledge and skills employers are looking for. Employers say they are having difficulty filling certain jobs related to technical skills, data analysis, and information technology. Young workers might put this to the test and ask employers to come together and work with local universities to design online courses and make them available to those who are underemployed but capable of handling introductory and advanced technical and leadership courses while working for them.

There is another dimension to what constitutes a good education today, namely learning to be creative, analytical, and able to solve problems individually and together with others. These are the behavioral skills that complement the technical and scientific knowledge that employers report they need in order to build high-performance organizations and support high-quality jobs. These skills seem to come more easily to young workers. The best schools—from elementary grades through college—have students working in teams and encourage creative problem-solving rather than rote memorization of facts and mathematical tables. The challenge lies in using these behavioral skills as complements to and not substitutes for mathematical, technical, and scientific knowledge needed in the jobs and organizations of the future. This could well be the next generation's way of becoming the "workers who give wisdom to these machines."

Where Will Their Bargaining Power Come From?

Taking these steps will equip the next-generation workforce with potentially their most important source of bargaining power: the knowledge, skills, and abilities needed to demand good-paying and fulfilling jobs. The best and most attractive employers will compete for employees with these skills and capabilities and will provide career pathways and the lifelong learning opportunities needed to keep these skills fresh. These employers will also provide opportunities to contribute to a sustainable and fulfilling organizational mission. The "Good Jobs" app mentioned in Chapter 4 showed that these are the features workers use to decide whether or not to accept a job offer. But what can workers do to ensure that these opportunities are not just limited to the isolated best high-road employers? What might they do to help make sure they become the norm?

Here is where the worker apps emerging out of the sharing economy might be used to enhance worker bargaining power and signal the need for more employers to adopt high-road strategies and practices. Apps such as Glassdoor, Turk Opticon, or Sherpashare might be a means for spreading these practices until they become the norm. We need to draw on these apps and develop additional ones and data sources that help workers find good jobs and good employers and avoid employers who are stuck on the low road.

Perhaps this is one of the things young workers can call for in the next-generation professional organizations and unions they might join and/or lead. When information is shared widely, the threat to employers of losing valuable employees and the ability to attract needed talent could become a key source of bargaining power and could incentivize more employers to either get on or stay on the high road.

But let the low-road bosses beware. Young workers are ready to stand together when they see injustice, unfairness, or unacceptable employment conditions being imposed on their peers. Remember the support workers and customers provided Market Basket employees when they were threatened by owners who might erode the high-road traditions and practices that served employees and customers so well! Remember United Students Against Sweatshops and their ability to stand up for decent labor standards for workers across the globe! The next-generation workforce will be better equipped than any in the past to stand in solidarity with all workers at home and across the globe. They will need to do so if the high road, fitted to the different circumstances, is to become the norm and spread at home and abroad.

Next-Generation Worker Organizations

Interests and Responsibilities

The primary responsibility of individual employee advocates is to increase job opportunities and improve the conditions of work for those they represent. But taken as a whole, the leaders of today and tomorrow's labor movement need to promote general improvements in job opportunities, working conditions, and social justice for all members of the workforce. Achieving these goals will require major transformations in strategy and practice that can reverse the long-term decline in union membership, expand the base of members and coalition partners, and develop new sources of power. This in turn will entail a wide range of experimentation in order to discover the mix of networks and organizations that are capable of recruiting, mobilizing, and sustaining members; discovering and sustaining new sources power and influence; and working collaboratively with employers, government leaders, and allied groups in civil society. In short, unions, in coalition with other progressive groups, need to once again become the economic engine for spreading high-road practices that will provide a foundation for the next-generation social contract.

Options and Actions

Independent, innovative, and powerful networks and organizations that mobilize and give workers a voice in things that are important to them are critical to building a new social contract. But the organizations that will help the next generation of workers gain a powerful voice cannot be built as a mirror image of the unions that were dominant in the mid-twentieth century and have declined in membership and influence.

Many innovative labor leaders have championed new models in recent years. But AFL-CIO president Richard Trumka's speech to the federation's 2013 convention gave a strong signal: The labor movement is ready and eager to experiment with new approaches. An excerpt of his speech is provided in Box 6.2.

Box 6.2

AFL-CIO president Richard Trumka on new labor strategies

It is time, my friends, to turn America right side up. And to turn America right side up, we need a real working class movement. And if that's going to happen, we—our institutions—have to do some things differently.

We must begin, here and now, today, the great work of reawakening a movement of working people—*all* working people, not just the people in this hall, not just the people we represent today—but everyone who works in this country, everyone who believes that people who work deserve to make enough to live and enjoy the good things in life.

We heard that all over America, workers are organizing in all kinds of ways, and they call their unity by all kinds of names—workers' unions, associations, centers, networks.

We heard that people want to be part of our movement but it's too hard to join—that we have to change so that our unions and our movement are open to everyone—to anyone who wants to join together for a better life. And today we're going to do that.

We heard that we have to change to reflect the times. The AFL and the CIO merged over 50 years ago, before the jumbo jet, before the cell phone, before the internet. We need to organize ourselves in ways that fit with the jobs people do now and how our economy works now.

And finally, we heard we have to make our unity real with action—we have to be able to organize on a large scale, in the workplace and in political life—quickly, efficiently, decisively. And with a strong, independent political voice.

And in everything we do, we have to join together with partners and allies who share our values and our vision for America. An America of shared prosperity. An America where you don't surrender your humanity, your dignity, your rights when you come to work. An America where we honor each individual, while understanding that connecting with each other, supporting each other—solidarity and community—are what give life meaning.

Throughout history, the energy and hopes of young workers have powered progress: If we are going to move forward, we must truly open our doors to the next generation.

If we are going to move forward, we must make our movement and our leadership as diverse as the workforce we speak for.

If we are going to move forward, we must move forward together—immigrants and the children of immigrants.

Source: "Remarks by AFL-CIO President Richard L. Trumka, 2013 AFL-CIO National Convention Keynote, Los Angeles, California," September 9, 2013, http://www.aflcio.org/Press-Room/Speeches/Remarks-by-AFL-CIO-President-Richard-L.Trumka-2013-AFL-CIO-National-Convention-Keynote-Los-Angeles-California.

Other innovative labor leaders are calling for and fostering experimentation with new models. I mentioned one example in Chapter 5. David Rolf, president of Service Employees International Union Local 775 in Seattle, has helped set up the Workers Lab, an "accelerator" that supports start-ups that apply the tools of business entrepreneurship to empower the next-generation workforce. His mantra is that these experiments have to build worker power in a modern way, grow to a scale large enough to have a national impact, and generate the resources needed to be sustainable. The Workers Lab hopes also hopes to foster invention of worker-centered apps that provide the information and support the networking workers need so they will know where the best job opportunities are and which employers to avoid. Professional organizations of all types can step up their advocacy, education and training, and certification programs to support the lifelong learning of their members. New inventions are likely to surface. The door is open for young worker entrepreneurs to put their creative minds and tools to work!

One of the lessons from our historical review in previous chapters is that we should never pronounce the labor movement dead. The industrial unions that emerged out of the ashes of the 1930s spurred both new and existing unions to adapt to the changing industrial order of the day. A similar rebirth is possible today. Unions that have invested heavily in the training and development of their members, from the traditional craft and occupational unions to broader-based unions in health care, are assets for workers, employers, and the economy. Unions that have demonstrated a willingness and a capacity to lead labor-management partnerships such as the one that was started at Saturn and the one that was carried forward at Kaiser Permanente have demonstrated their value: Their members have had a voice in driving improvements in productivity, quality, and customer service. Similar partnerships are now under way in education with the active financial and leadership support of the National Education Association and the American Federation of Teachers, the nation's two large teachers' unions.

A key lesson learned from these innovative models is that labor needs to champion and support these partnerships and that eventually government labor policy needs to catch up with and endorse this model of labor-management relations.

Future partnership models could take many different forms, including works councils in specific enterprises such as the one that the UAW and Volkswagen are attempting to create in Tennessee, frontline teams such as those that developed at Kaiser Permanente, occupational forums and networks, and industry and community partnerships with educational institutions and employers. The dominant image of unions and professional associations needs to become one of forward-looking innovators who are interested in strategies that include partnerships with a variety of stakeholders.

Yet it is clear that the advice to "trust but keep your powder dry" still applies. The campaigns of fast-food workers and other campaigns that seek to give voice and the right to representation to workers in low-wage jobs, immigrants, and others who are subject to mistreatment must be a central part of labor's mission and strategy. Partnerships with willing employers are sustainable only if there is an understanding that the alternative is labor's willingness and ability to draw on more traditional sources of power to protect and advance member interests. These more traditional pressure tactics will need to be used in dealing with employers who oppose the efforts of workers to gain representation or who choose to keep unions or professional associations at arm's length.

Building Alliances

The large number of diverse community-based organizations that are already active in advocating for worker rights and interests also have important roles to play, especially in supporting efforts to improve conditions for low-wage workers, immigrants, and others who face multiple challenges at work and at home. Some of these are working in loose coalitions with existing unions and some operate on their own or in coalitions with consumers or local like-minded groups and leaders. The efforts to organize fast-food workers that have sprung up across the country, the efforts of organizations such as the Restaurant Opportunities Centers United that stress good food and good working conditions for those who prepare and serve it, and the worker centers supported by Interfaith Worker Justice that combine a commitment to faith-based social justice with campaigns to end wage theft are all examples of work that needs to continue to grow and be supported by workers and citizens across the occupational and income spectrums. And the AFL-CIO is putting its efforts where Rich Trumka's rhetoric suggests it needs to go. By supporting a Young Workers Group,[3] it seeks to ensure that the next generation will lead the way in shaping the labor movement of the future!

The online education arena is an untapped potential resource that labor can use to expand the educational services it provides to members. Labor could take a page from business's playbook by negotiating group discounts for online courses that generate certificates or credits toward advanced degrees. This is, in essence, what the WorkAmerica project mentioned in Chapter 5 is trying to do. Making lifelong learning of members a key component of unions might be one way for them to build a sustainable financial and membership growth model.

Educators

Educators have two primary goals and responsibilities: to teach students to be literate and informed citizens and to ensure that the workforce of the future has the knowledge, skills, and abilities to compete in a global,

---

[3] http://www.aflcio.org/Get-Involved/Young-Workers.

knowledge-driven economy. Today these responsibilities begin in early childhood and extend through the full working careers of the adult labor force. Given the importance of education and skill to an economy based on knowledge and innovation, educators of all sorts and levels, from those who teach in preschools to those who teach in lifelong-learning programs, need to be active contributors to the next-generation social contract.

Options and Actions

I recently found myself sitting at a luncheon between two young mothers who were visiting MIT from China and Portugal. Our conversation turned to when their children started going to school. The Chinese mother said that all children go to state-supported programs as soon after birth as their parents will send them. The Portuguese mother said that all children start government-supported pre-kindergarten programs at age three.

Rarely is there such a universal agreement as there is about the notion that providing early childhood educational opportunities to all children and families pays off for individuals in the form of future earnings and for society in the form of lower welfare benefits and crime rates. This idea is backed by strong research evidence. Preparing the workforce of the future (and the solid citizens of the future) starts at this tender stage. If America has any hope of having a world-class workforce in the future, it has to start now by investing in access to preschool for all. Perhaps leaders in our major cities and selected states will lead the way in filling the vacuum in affordable and high-quality pre-kindergarten programs for all the children of the next-generation parents.

The pace of innovations in elementary and secondary education is accelerating across the nation. President Obama's Race to the Top initiative may go down in history as one of his administration's signal achievements. It provides both the carrots and the sticks needed to get teachers and their unions, school administrators, and school board members focused on a clear and singular goal—improving student achievement. At the same time, this government initiative has avoided taking sides in the divisive and misguided battle over whether to support, limit, or oppose the growth of private schools in general and charter schools in particular. It is clear that a mix of public, religious, and secular private schools is healthy for the nation. Catholic schools do some of the best work for young children and families in impoverished urban neighborhoods. Charter schools have provided models for public schools to emulate in reforming their approaches to teaching, opening up opportunities for young dedicated teachers, holding principals and teachers accountable for job performance, and reforming and extending the hours children have available for learning and/or enriching after-school experiences.

Yet the vast majority of young people will continue to attend and depend on public schools. That is why the collaborative initiatives of teachers' unions and school districts that are now under way around the country need to become the norm in public education. Many young teachers are leading this effort and are eager to be joined by future cohorts. Note to teacher unions and school district officials: Don't keep the next generation teachers of waiting to put their skills, energies, new ideas, and leadership potential to work!

I have already noted the key roles community colleges and universities play in building alliances with employers and labor and other employee groups to provide online and in-person educational offerings tailored to the learning styles of adult students. These alliances foster employment opportunities, work to address skill shortages in the workforce, and provide opportunities to upgrade the nation's stock of human capital. Colleges and universities need to meet the ongoing needs of their alumni and others who are interested in and able to engage with online courses from wherever they are situated across the world. Let's hope that this is just the tip of the iceberg in what could become the next-generation model for lifelong learning around the globe.

Next-Generation Business Schools

If you stroll through the MIT Sloan School of Management's new building and look up on the wall you will see the school's mission boldly displayed: "To produce principled innovative leaders who improve the world." A laudable aspiration and mission! Who could disagree? But here's what one Sloan MBA student said in a focus group interview when she was asked what she thought: "The mission is everywhere in the marketing of Sloan but nowhere to be found in the core curriculum." Another said "What principles are we talking about?"

The point that these and others are making is that the core curriculum of Sloan and just about all other leading business and management schools in the United States is dominated by a narrow, technical, finance-driven model of management and the role of the corporation in society. It reflects and reinforces the short-term shareholder-based view of the firm. But this was not always the case in business schools, nor need it be so in the future. Rakesh Khurana of Harvard Business School drove this point home clearly in his book on how business schools gradually gave up on the stated mission of their founders to educate and graduate leaders who would hold business to a higher professional standard, both on technical and scientific grounds and on normative grounds that recognized that business leaders have an obligation to society.[4] This original mission slowly got pushed aside as the financialization of the firm came to dominate business practices in the 1980s. Today finance departments are typically the most powerful group in business schools, just as finance departments are the most powerful group in corporations.

Business schools need to change. They may already be changing at the margins. One supportive ally in this process is the Aspen Institute. Among other things, it supports the development and dissemination of case studies that illustrate corporate social responsibility. Each year it gives a set of awards to leading business professors who do research and teaching that embody social responsibility principles and tools. This is a good thing, and it has helped introduce more of these ideas into the curriculum of a number of business schools.

There is also a growing number of elective courses in management schools that take on a broader perspective. One of the most popular is taught at Harvard Business School by one of its most talented teachers, Rebecca Henderson. She chose the audacious title "Reimagining Capitalism" to describe her course. At Sloan we teach a similar course with the less catchy title of "Managing Sustainable Businesses for People and Profits."

---

[4] Rakesh Khurana, *From Higher Aims to Hired Hands: The Social Transformation of American Business Schools and the Unfulfilled Promise of Management as a Profession* (Princeton, NJ: Princeton University Press, 2010).

We only reach a small fraction of the MBA student body, but those who take the course are passionate about getting their peers exposed to the choices leaders have about whether to adopt high- or low-road strategies.

Students respond well to these courses. But they point out a problem with this approach. These elective courses only capture the attention of the self-selected students who already are inclined to have an open mind to these issues. They argue that if the basic culture of business schools is to be changed and future business organizations are to be managed in fundamentally new ways, all students needed to be exposed to these ideas, to alternative tools of management, and to the best way to implement such management strategies. So I asked the MBAs who took this class in 2015 what to do to expose their peers to the choices they have as business leaders in deciding whether to adopt high- or low-road strategies. Here's a sample of their thoughts:

> The topic of how to manage the next generation workforce is of critical importance. Regardless of whether we want to confront reality, the fact remains that as the workers driving the American workforce change, the workforce will rapidly shift to a new set of skills, values, behaviors, and expectations. While some traditional management practices will continue to apply, many other practices will need to be tweaked, revised, or reconsidered altogether. If Sloan is going to prepare its students to be management leaders of the future, it must . . . integrate lessons learned from this class and ones like it throughout the entire curriculum.

> Another idea would be to offer a program or a few courses which, when taken together, offer the student an official certification of some kind: a "Future High Road Manager" certificate. By offering an added incentive (the certificate) for the student to engage more with this type of material by taking extra classes, more students' interests would be peaked and you could reach more of them.

> The material in this class should be positioned to not only facilitate dialogue and awareness around MIT but also use the lessons in the classroom to help underemployed and marginalized workers in and around Boston. For this reason, I believe the course

should evolve to a module that will challenge Sloan students to execute a real world plan of action to improve millennial employment in greater Boston. This lab offering will be a way for Sloanies to directly put into action what they have learned during their coursework and use their vast repository of knowledge and experience to impact the lives of others.

One approach to implementing the students' suggestions is illustrated in the week-long integrated exercise we use at Sloan to begin our part-time Executive MBA program. We take Walmart's sustainability initiative as a case study and have faculty teach it from their different disciplinary or functional perspectives. One of us teaches the case from the perspective of employees and communities and others examine it from finance/shareholder, marketing/consumer, operations, strategy, and global management perspectives. Then teams in the class are tasked with putting together reports to Walmart's "Board of Directors" (faculty directors of the program play this role with great skill) about whether Walmart should alter its sustainability strategy in any way.

This is one way to embed these concepts, tools, and multiple normative perspectives into the core curriculum right up front in a management program. And thanks go to Walmart for providing such a vivid, extreme case. Now if only they would send a cohort to Sloan to go through this exercise and see what they might learn and then do differently!

A growing number of MBA students who share these views are banding together in a cross-university club known as Net Impact.[5] It has attracted over 50,000 participants so far who meet at least once a year to compare notes and share ideas about how to get more environmental and social sustainability content into their school's curriculum. So MBA students of the future, keep leading the way in demanding these courses and creating the social and professional networks that will make this the defining feature of your cohort—even better than the HBS class of 1949!

Business school faculty and deans can also provide leadership in mobilizing and coordinating some of the local business, labor, government, and community leader forums and networks that will be needed to overcome

---

[5] https://netimpact.org/.

the institutional gulf that has grown up between these parties in recent years. We have experimented with bringing these types of multi-stakeholder groups together at MIT. Other schools, such as the University of Massachusetts-Boston, have gone a step further by engaging students and faculty to do research on organizational and social change projects with firms and nonprofits in the region. More of this type of action learning and support for local innovation is needed around the country.

Government Leaders

The primary responsibilities of government leaders with respect to work are to manage macroeconomic policies to promote job growth and employment continuity, enact and enforce employment policies that balance the needs and interests of workers and employers in ways that align with the nation's values and public interests, and promote and support innovations in employment practices that enhance productivity and good jobs.

Options and Actions

Washington has to finally start doing its job. We need to elect and appoint national leaders who are driven by a commitment to serving the national interest by working together across party lines to regain the confidence and respect of the public and break the partisan gridlock that is now paralyzing government. We have learned that most national policy innovations are first incubated and tested at local or state levels or in the private sector. There now are multiple examples to build on if and when Washington is ready to raise the national minimum wage, introduce family and/or paid sick leave, strengthen community colleges and related training institutions through the types of consortia we know work well, expand investments in infrastructure, and so forth. Hopefully, the local- and state-level leaders who successfully champion these efforts will take their ideas and experiences to Washington.

Building on these local examples would be a good starting point. But nothing short of a major transformation of current labor and employment policies, leadership, and enforcement will be adequate. So I complete the call to action with a blueprint for federal action that is based on the lessons from the New Deal and on more recent local innovations and is informed by the basic assumptions of the next-generation social contract.

Macroeconomic Policies: Investing for the Future

We have to start with macroeconomic policy. Here we definitely need to take to heart the central macroeconomic policy lesson of the 1930s. It took the massive investment of the government in gearing up production for World War II to end the Great Depression. Now, in the twenty-first century, it will take an infusion of sustained investment—perhaps a mix of public and private dollars—to finally meet the nation's needs for more high-quality jobs.

One of the best investments government could make would be to begin rebuilding America's deteriorating infrastructure. The American Society of Civil Engineers estimates that America has a $3 trillion backlog of repairs to the nation's infrastructure. Conservative economists such as Martin Feldstein, liberals such as Paul Krugman, and many in between endorse this strategy for creating jobs and energizing the economy.

The reason there is such broad-based support for infrastructure investments is that they generate positive long-run economic returns and create good jobs. Berkeley economist Laura Tyson estimates that an investment of $100 billion would generate approximately two million jobs. Thus, an investment of $50 billion per year through the rest of this decade would produce four million new jobs.[6] Moreover, many of these jobs would be good ones, requiring middle-skill apprenticeship or equivalent technical training and/or professional engineering or management degrees.

Most of the proposals for an infrastructure initiative call for a mixture of private and public capital as the initial source of funds. If, as appears to be the case, Congress is unwilling to act on its own, the private sector could take the lead in raising at least some of the necessary capital. The labor movement announced in 2011 that it is prepared to commit up to $10 billion in pension funds to an infrastructure initiative. Given their special interest in reducing uncertainty, Wall Street firms could be

---

[6] Laura D. Tyson, "A Better Stimulus Plan for the U.S.," *Harvard Business Review* 89, nos. 1–2 (2011): 53.

called on to build a substantially larger pool of funds. Then business and labor could jointly propose that government further leverage these funds in ways that lower the effective interest rate costs associated with infrastructure projects. Having business and labor as co-investors has another potential benefit. Their joint oversight could help ensure that the organizations carrying out this work adopt state-of-the-art employment practices and the high standards necessary for ensuring that these will be high-quality jobs and projects that will be managed efficiently and completed on time, safely, and on budget.

This way we get both the sustained economic stimulus that is needed and a demonstration of how business and labor can rise to the occasion and work together in a sustained way on a project of significant national interest. They have done so in the past during world wars and in the space race that met President Kennedy's goal of putting a man on the moon before the end of the decade. They needed and got a good deal of help from neutral mediators, arbitrators, and facilitators along the way. Are today's business, labor, and neutral professionals up to the equivalent task? They might just be if whoever is in the White House puts his or her reputation on the line and supports the effort.

Infrastructure is only one potentially attractive investment opportunity. Equally important for building an innovation economy would be restoring investments in science and engineering to the levels of previous decades. MIT president Rafael Reif has been a consistent and articulate advocate for government investment in scientific research.

Innovation is fueled by a long-time partnership between the federal government and the nation's scientists and engineers. Since World War II, federal funding for science has led to important technological breakthroughs and contributed mightily to our national defense. Over the long term, as much as three-quarters of economic growth may be attributable to innovation and technological change. . . . [But] federal R&D as a percentage of GDP—essentially, our societal commitment to research—has fallen from 1.3 percent in 1979 to 0.8 percent in 2013. Our competitors are going in the other direction.[7]

---

[7] L. Rafael Reif, "The Innovation Deficit," *The Boston Globe*, December 29, 2013, K8.

In summary, the first order of business for the federal government is to make the investments needed to support economic growth and to do so in ways that lay the foundation for a globally competitive, innovation-driven economy. But macroeconomic strategies alone are not enough. The legacy of work and employment policies and enforcement models that have carried over from the industrial economy of the twentieth century also need to be updated to better match today's economy, workforce, and work arrangements.

Bringing Employment Policies into the Twenty-First Century

Recall that Frances Perkins told President Roosevelt that if he hired her as his secretary of labor, she would fight for the policies she wanted. When he gave her the green light to pursue that agenda, she turned to a cadre of experts who had direct experience in designing and working with state and local innovations that served as the model for the New Deal. We will need an equivalent infusion of expertise and experience to advise the president and advocate with Congress for a set of new employment policies and enforcement strategies tailored to the needs of the next generation and the economy. The good news is a large army of academic, industry, labor, and community professionals have built up this knowledge and experience by helping craft and evaluate experiments in local governments and in the private sector over the past decade. Much of their work is presented and can be found on the website of the network they formed, the Employment Policy Research Network (www.employmentpolicy.org), or on the site that grew out of the online course I taught at MIT (www.speakupforwork.com). Think tanks with varying political leanings such as the Economic Policy Institute, the Center for Economic and Policy Research, the Center for American Progress, New America, the Brookings Institution, the American Enterprise Institute, The Heritage Foundation, and the Cato Institute have become important reservoirs for data, analysis, and policy ideas. Let's put this knowledge and research to work!

A good place to start would be filling the biggest and most embarrassing gap in national policy—something all American families have a stake in filling. I'll describe it through a bet that I unfortunately won. In 2005 I made a bet with Marian Baird, a good friend who was visiting MIT from the University of Sydney. We share an interest in work and family policies and lamented that at that time Australia and the United States were the only two highly developed countries in the world without some form of paid family or parental leave. So we made a bet: Which country would be the last? We each were pessimistic enough to place our bet on our home countries. Marian, however, decided this was a bet she wanted to lose and went back to Australia and worked day and night to lay the intellectual foundation for the maternity leave policy the Australian government enacted in 2012. Marian's reward for losing the bet: She was named one of Australia's 100 most influential women in 2013. My reward for winning the bet: I was stuck with a version of the winner's curse. Now only the United States has the distinction of being the last holdout against a national policy that supports working parents with newborns.

Three states—New Jersey, California, and Rhode Island—have taken the lead in enacting forms of paid family leave. California enacted paid family leave in 2004. A 2010 follow-up study by Eileen Appelbaum and Ruth Milkman on the effects of the new benefit reported these findings:

> PFL [Paid Family Leave] use is associated with better economic, social, and health outcomes for workers and their families. . . . Workers in low-quality jobs who used PFL were more likely than those who did not use it to return to the same employer after a family leave, were more satisfied with the length of their leaves, were better able to care for newborns, and were better able to make childcare arrangements.

The study found that despite strong opposition to passage of the PFL bill by employers, five years after implementation,

> the new PFL program was a "nonevent" for the vast majority of businesses. Our data reveal that employers themselves report that the PFL had no effect or a positive effect on the productivity, profitability or performance, turnover, and worker morale of their organizations. Moreover many employers enjoyed cost savings as a result of the program, and abuse was rare.[8]

---

[8] Eileen Appelbaum and Ruth Milkman, *Unfinished Business: Paid Family Leave in California and the Future of U.S. Work-Family Policy* (Ithaca, NY: Cornell University/ILR

One limitation of the program, however, was that many low-income workers were unaware of it or were afraid that using it would jeopardize their future employment. The implication is that even with legislation like this, community, immigrant, labor, and other groups need to educate workers about gaining access to benefits they are entitled to use and support them in their efforts to do so.

Now it is time to learn from these state experiences and from careful studies of private-sector firms that have demonstrated the value of flexible work and family programs and practices.[9] Putting this issue at the top of the employment policy priority list would send a strong signal that the focus of debate will be on the workforce and the economy as we find it today, not on tired debates that repeat past battles between traditional labor and business groups.

The old social contract was based on a long-term employment relationship with an employer that provided an extensive array of benefits that included health insurance and a pension plan. Today's employment relationships are more diverse, more uncertain in duration, and increasingly do not come with either of these traditional benefits, or if they do, a higher portion of the costs and risks have been shifted to employees.

Another aspect of our outdated policies harkens back to what I earlier described as a major achievement of the World War II–era National War Labor Board: namely, encouraging firms to provide health and retirement benefits. That strategy worked brilliantly as long as workers stayed with a single employer for most of their careers. Clearly those days are over. But alternatives are not yet in place that are as effective in ensuring against the risk of individual or family illness or injury or that would help workers save for a secure retirement income.

Press, 2010). For another study of the effects of this law that reported similar findings, see Charles J. Baum and Christopher J. Ruhn, "The Effects of Paid Family Leave on Labor Market Outcomes," National Bureau of Economic Research Working Paper 19741, December 2013, http://www.nber.org/papers/w19741.

[9] See Lotte Bailyn, *Breaking the Mold: Redesigning Work for Productive and Satisfying Lives*, 2nd ed. (Ithaca, NY: Cornell University/ILR Press, 2006); and Erin L. Kelly, Phyllis Moen, and Eric Tranby, "Changing Workplaces to Reduce Work-Family Conflict: Schedule Control in a White-Collar Organization," *American Sociological Review* 76, no. 2 (2011): 265–290.

The enactment of the Affordable Care Act (colloquially known as Obamacare) is the first major step toward weaning ourselves away from employers as the primary providers of health insurance. But the new program is only a first step, not a final solution. This point was brought home at the annual meeting of the National Academy of Human Resources, a gathering that brings together the top human resources executives in the country. How the new Obamacare legislation would affect their firms in the short run and over the course of the decade was fresh in their minds and was a major topic of discussion at the meeting. Two points of consensus emerged from the discussion: (1) their firms had no plans for improving their health care benefit offerings—all were looking for strategies to further cut costs or shift a higher percentage of the costs to current or retired employees; and (2) these executives predicted that by the end of this decade their firms would be out of the health insurance business altogether. Unfortunately, none of the executives suggested a plan for how to turn their predictions into reality by the end of the decade.

The retirement issue is more dire. Social Security, the baseline, near-universal retirement system, continues in place but will need some adjustments if it is to stay solvent for the next generation. This is not an insurmountable challenge—some combination of relaxing the income limits on social security contributions, increasing the eligibility age modestly to account for longer life expectancies, and/or modifying the cost of living or some other aspect of the benefit formula can assure long-term solvency. This will take political courage, to be sure—after all, Social Security is not called the third rail of politics for nothing.

The bigger problem is that the private pension system that emerged during and after World War II and was a key part of the old social contract is dying a slow but steady death. At its highest point, in the 1970s, it covered just under half of the labor force. Now less than 20 percent of the workforce has some form of defined benefit plan. Most of these are public-sector employees. Many private employers have dumped these plans. In their place, some have offered 401ks or some other form of defined contribution plan, but these are not filling the retirement security gap. As we saw with the Great Recession, these funds are subject to higher risk of losing value when economic growth slows or declines.

That means that they reduce incentives for individuals to retire and draw on them just when we most want workers to retire—when the economy is in trouble and young people are having the most difficulty finding a job! 401ks are not a substitute for a real retirement saving plan. They are a useful supplement, but they have not and will not serve as an adequate retirement program for the next generation. Something else is needed.

The good news: A simple solution has been proposed by Teresa Ghilarducci, a faculty member at the New School for Social Research. She outlines it in a book with the catchy title of *When I'm Sixty-Four.*[10] Her plan calls for employees to contribute 5 percent of their income, part of which could be paid by their employer. The savings would be put into a government-administered fund and the government would guarantee a minimum annual 3 percent rate of return on the invested funds that would then turn into a lifetime annuity at retirement age. This proposal deals with many of the problems associated with the decline of traditional pension plans and the inadequate 401ks or similar plans. Professor Ghilarducci's plan does not depend on individual employers to provide a pension program, it does not shift all the risk of retirement savings to individuals, it does not create the perverse cyclical retirement disincentive, and, like Social Security, it is universal in coverage regardless of the type of employment relationship (including independent contractors) one has at various points in his or her career.

This is one well-thought-out option for meeting the retirement security needs of the next generation. Others might be invented. Or we could take an even easier route by simply expanding coverage and increasing the benefit levels of Social Security. The task today is to squarely face the need for a stable, universal, and adequate supplement to or increase in Social Security. The baby boom generation benefited from decisive actions taken by President Roosevelt and his advisors in 1935. We need to take a similar action now or these same baby boomers who benefited from Roosevelt's actions had better be prepared to subsidize their children's retirement or leave many of them to retire into poverty.

[10] Teresa Ghilarducci, *When I'm Sixty-Four: The Plot Against Pensions and the Plan to Save Them* (Princeton, NJ: Princeton University Press, 2008).

From Responsible Employers to the Fissured Workplace

In the heyday of the old social contract, most people could tell you who they worked for and have no doubts about it. They worked for GM or IBM or the local department store, gas station, insurance company, hotel, utility company, and so on. Today ask someone who helps install cell towers, works in a big brand-name hotel, or services your home Internet connection who he or she works for and you are likely to get a wide variety of answers. And if you ask their employer who is responsible for enforcing core labor standards related to workplace safety and health, wage payment and overtime rules, and equal employment opportunity, you are likely to get even more ambiguous answers. This is why when bad things such as the Gulf Coast oil spill happen, even big companies such as British Petroleum (BP) (the owners of the well with rights to the oil that spilled), Halliburton (the contractor that provided testing services related to the stability of the drilling process), and Transocean (the company that provided the drilling platform) each pointed the finger at the others in efforts to shirk responsibility for the accident and the financial liabilities it generated.

David Weil is the nation's leading academic expert (and now thankfully also the administrator of the Wage and Hour Division of the U.S. Department of Labor) on what he calls the "fissured workplace" and how to update enforcement of basic employment standards to adapt to these new organizational realities.[11] He notes that for most hotels, the name on the marquee may not be the company that owns the property, a different company may manage the specific facility, and many of the tasks related to running the hotel such as housecleaning may be contracted out to yet another company. Moreover, these properties and management contracts change periodically so that the mix of employers is in constant flux.

Weil and others who have studied this problem argue that changes in both legislation and enforcement strategies are needed to adapt to these fissured employment relationships. The legislative change is clear and is already being tested in a few states such as California, New York, and Illinois. The idea is simple and direct: Hold the firm that purchases the ultimate goods or services or sets the standards for the work responsible

---

[11] David Weil, *The Fissured Workplace* (Cambridge, MA: Harvard University Press, 2014).

for assuring that basic employment laws and standards are met by all firms and contractors that contribute to the product or service. So in the case of the Gulf Oil disaster, BP would have been the responsible employer. If a policy of holding the ultimate purchaser of goods and services responsible had been in place, BP likely would have taken more care to ensure that its managers controlled key decisions. Because such a policy was not in place, some of these decisions fell between the cracks of shared or ambiguous authority and reporting relationships. Investigators later found that the absence of clear channels of responsibility was the root cause of the accident. The same assignment of responsibility would be true of the giant oil and chemical companies that subcontract some of the most dangerous maintenance work when they retool parts of their refineries and processing plants. The same assignment of responsibility would be true of AT&T and other cell phone service providers when they issue contracts and subcontracts to specialized firms that build their cell towers. And the same would be true when Hilton or Marriott or Starwoods contracts with others to manage a hotel property bearing its name.

The enforcement strategy Weil endorses relies on a mix of carrots and sticks. It would reward firms that have high standards and workplace practices that achieve high compliance (that is, low violation rates) and would target enforcement resources on the most egregious violators of employment standards. Making this work will require better and more coordinated information gathering and sharing of knowledge of violation and compliance rates across different government agencies such as the Occupational Safety and Health Administration (OSHA), the Equal Employment Opportunity Commission (EEOC), the National Labor Relations Board (NLRB), and the Wage and Hour Division of the Labor Department—the alphabet soup of quasi-independent government agencies that enforce different labor standards. It would also require that these agencies work with and empower community groups, unions and professional associations, immigrant organizations, and individual workers to report violations, complement the work of enforcement agencies by monitoring workplace practices, and work cooperatively with employers to ensure compliance and gradually upgrade standards so their workplaces can move from the targeted to the rewarded side of the enforcement ledger.

The government needs to set the example. A *New York Times* front-page headline announced in December 2013 that the agencies of the federal government are among the biggest purchasers of goods made in sweatshops around the world.[12] The president needs to assign responsibility to a single high-level official for creating, monitoring, and enforcing the government's own code of conduct throughout its supply chain. It is time for the government to learn from the work that has already been done by private firms and the multi-stakeholder groups that are actively addressing this issue in global supply chains.

In 1965, President Lyndon Johnson signed an executive order that required all federal contractors to demonstrate that they were taking affirmative action to end discrimination in their employment practices. An equivalent executive order that would require all federal contractors to demonstrate that they are taking affirmative action to enforce the full array of labor standards and pay fair wages would go a long way toward supporting and broadly diffusing the high-road strategies needed to support the next-generation social contract.

And Yes, We Do Need a New Labor Policy

Just as the National Labor Relations Act was the most contentious part of the New Deal legislation in the 1930s, so too are debates today over how to replace the nation's defunct labor law. Let there be no doubt: the old National Labor Relations Act is "ossified," as labor law expert Cynthia Estlund has so accurately described it.[13] For years, the law has failed to deliver on its promise of providing workers access to collective bargaining, as a national commission noted 20 years ago. John Paul Ferguson's work on this topic was summarized in Chapter 5. What he found is worth repeating here: Less than one in ten organizing efforts succeeds in getting a labor contract if management opposes the organizing effort. This is the case even when a majority of workers indicate that they want

---

[12] Ian Urbina, "The U.S. Flouts Its Own Advice in Procuring Overseas Clothing," *New York Times*, December 22, 2013, http://www.nytimes.com/2013/12/23/world/americas/buying-overseas-clothing-us-flouts-its-own-advice.html?_r=0.

[13] Cynthia Estlund, *Regoverning the Workplace* (New Haven, CT: Yale University Press, 2010).

to be represented by a union. The bottom line is that today any employer who wants to oppose efforts to organize a union through legal or illegal means has about a 90 percent chance of succeeding. That means that today it is no longer workers who decide whether or not they will have an independent voice at work. Lawyers, consultants, and their employer control this decision. That was not the intent of the National Labor Relations Act when it was enacted!

The problem is even deeper. The many adversarial doctrines, traditions, and norms that built up in traditional collective bargaining over the last 80 years no longer produce a competitive or happy workplace. The high-performance workplaces discussed throughout this book are either nonunion or are unionized settings in which management and labor leaders work together in partnerships that ignore or put aside many (if not all) of the old doctrines and traditions. Adversarial labor-management relationships can no longer compete with these alternatives.

A modern labor policy therefore has to have two equally important objectives: (1) to restore the ability of workers to gain an independent and effective voice at work; and (2) to promote collaborative forms of worker voice and engagement that serve the mutual interests of the workforce, employers, and the clients, customers, patients, students, or other ultimate consumers they serve.

Here again the seeds of an innovative labor policy have been sown by the companies that have implemented different types of partnerships. Saturn and Kaiser Permanente represent the most comprehensive and perhaps most complex models. Ford and the UAW have fashioned an approach that works for them, as have Southwest Airlines and its unions. Volkswagen and the UAW are experimenting with yet another model based on the German works council system. A number of hotels and the workers' organization UNITE HERE have reached agreements on the partnership approach in their industry. The key strategy lies in government endorsement of these new approaches and in opening up labor law and policy to more of this type of experimentation. This will take leadership and outreach by the government's chief labor officer—the secretary of labor.

There is precedent for the secretary of labor to play this role. Frances Perkins had a vision for what was needed in the New Deal and was given the opportunity to pursue it. Later secretaries under both Republican administrations, such as George Shultz (Nixon administration) and

John Dunlop and William Usery (Ford administration), and Democratic administrations, such as Arthur Goldberg (Kennedy administration), Willard Wirtz (Johnson administration), Ray Marshall (Carter administration), and Robert Reich (Clinton administration), were influential and visible advocates for innovations in labor and employment policies. Each actively engaged with and enlisted the advice and support of labor and business leaders to address the key employment challenges of their day. Tom Perez, the labor secretary President Obama appointed in 2013, has taken up this mantle as well.

This tradition is harder to pursue today, given the diversity of voices that would need to be engaged. We can no longer simply bring "labor" and "business" together. Today "labor" means both leaders of established unions and professional associations and leaders of working women's organizations, immigrant groups, associations of independent contractors, and others and "business" is comprised of an equally diverse group of large and small employers, multinational firms and local and regional business groups, and so forth. So no single national committee is likely to suffice or be able to reach some rarified consensus over all of the policy issues that need to be updated and transformed. Instead, what we need is an era of sustained dialogue and engagement, evidence-based experimentation, and testing at the national, sectoral, and regional levels. In short, we need a national champion and proactive social engineer to rebuild the dialogue across the key stakeholders who need to be part of the process of forging and sustaining the next-generation social contract.

This is arguably a very ambitious and far-reaching agenda for transforming labor and employment policy. But anything less will likely fail to provide the equivalent of the New Deal platform on which the old social contract was built gradually over subsequent decades. While this agenda is ambitious, it is also entirely doable. The ideas and actions outlined here are all derived from experimentation that was done in the private sector or in state or local government. Some come from the research and ideas of academics, but none come from ivory-towered theorists who are far removed from the practical world of work. The ideas come from evidence generated from field studies of what is working on a small scale. Now is the time to test these on a scale large enough to meet the needs of the next generation.

An Invitation to Action

The public is clearly ready for a more proactive, inclusive strategy. As noted in Chapter 1, income inequality is now recognized as a serious national (indeed global) moral and economic problem. Wages are on the table for discussion and recent efforts to increase minimums by states, local governments, and private businesses have been well received by the public. Editorial writers of varying political persuasions are for the first time in memory writing about the need to increase workers' bargaining power and rebuild unions. Perhaps we are about to open another window of opportunity to break the Washington gridlock on work and employment policy. I hope so. It might just be the last chance baby boomers have to save themselves from the dismal legacy they are about to leave their children and grandchildren. So time is of the essence.

Let's all get to work.

Index

THE GIVING VOICE TO VALUES ON BUSINESS ETHICS AND CORPORATE SOCIAL RESPONSIBILITY COLLECTION

Mary Gentile, Editor

The Giving Voice To Values initiative teamed up with Business Expert Press to produce a collection of books on Business Ethics and Corporate Social Responsibility that will bring a practical, solutions-oriented, skill-building approach to the salient questions of values-driven leadership. Giving Voice To Values (www.GivingVoiceToValues.org)—the curriculum, the pedagogy and the research upon which it is based—was designed to transform the foundational assumptions upon which the teaching of business ethics is based, and importantly, to equip future business leaders to not only know what is right, but how to make it happen.

Other Titles in This Collection

- *Ethical Leadership in Sport: What's Your ENDgame?* by Pippa Grange
- *The ART of Responsible Communication: Leading With Values Every Day* by David L. Remund
- *Engaging Millennials for Ethical Leadership: What Works For Young Professionals and Their Managers* by Jessica McManus Warnell
- *Sales Ethics: How To Sell Effectively While Doing the Right Thing* by Alberto Aleo and Alice Alessandri
- *Working Ethically in Finance: Clarifying Our Vocation* by Anthony Asher
- *A Strategic and Tactical Approach to Global Business Ethics, Second Edition* by Lawrence A. Beer

Forthcoming Titles in This Collection

- *War Stories: Fighting, Competing, Imagining, Leading* by Leigh Hafrey
- *Leadership Ethics: Moral Power for Business Leaders* by Lindsay Thompson

Announcing the Business Expert Press Digital Library

Concise e-books business students need for classroom and research

This book can also be purchased in an e-book collection by your library as

- a one-time purchase,
- that is owned forever,
- allows for simultaneous readers,
- has no restrictions on printing, and
- can be downloaded as PDFs from within the library community.

Our digital library collections are a great solution to beat the rising cost of textbooks. E-books can be loaded into their course management systems or onto students' e-book readers.

The **Business Expert Press** digital libraries are very affordable, with no obligation to buy in future years. For more information, please visit **www.businessexpertpress.com/librarians**. To set up a trial in the United States, please email **sales@businessexpertpress.com**

CPSIA information can be obtained
at www.ICGtesting.com
Printed in the USA
FFOW05n2227291215

9 781631 574016